Red
China

An Asian View

Red China

An
Asian View

by Sripati Chandra-sekhar

FREDERICK A. PRAEGER, *Publisher*
New York

BOOKS THAT MATTER

Published in the United States of America in 1961
by Frederick A. Praeger, Inc., Publisher
64 University Place, New York 3, N.Y.

Library of Congress Catalog Card Number: 61-9880

THIRD PRINTING, 1962

RED CHINA: AN ASIAN VIEW
is published in two editions:
A Praeger Paperback (PPS-42)
A clothbound edition

Manufactured in the United States of America

This book is Number 92
in the series of
Praeger Publications in Russian History and World Communism.

To my sister SHRIDEVI

Foreword

According to the *United Nations Demographic Yearbook* published in August, 1960, there are about 2,900,000,000 people in the world, and some 48,000,000 more are added every year. Oddly enough, Africa, now very much in the news, is the most prolific continent with an average birth rate of forty-five per thousand as compared to Europe's average birth rate of only nineteen per thousand. Population, today, is intimately connected with politics and economics, and it therefore greatly influences the progress of both. According to the *Yearbook*, more than half the world's inhabitants live in four countries—China (669,000,000), India (403,000,000), the Soviet Union (209,000,000), and the United States (178,000,000).

It is in light of these significant figures that Dr. Sripati Chandra-sekhar's analytical and perceptive book on China should be read. As a well-known demographer, Dr. Chandra-sekhar has made a close study of the population problems of many countries, particularly in Asia. Though not intimately associated with the political world, he is, as are all individuals of any awareness today, interested in political problems, particularly in their relation to demographic trends, and it is in this context that his book deserves to be read closely by both the expert and the lay reader.

Dr. Chandra-sekhar had the advantage of visiting China both under the Kuomintang regime, when the Chinese government was fighting desperately on two fronts—against Japan and against its own indigenous Communists—and also after the Communists had replaced the Kuomintang on the mainland of China. This book is concerned with his latter visit.

vii

The author traveled a great deal throughout the country and was able to see and observe its developments not only in the social but also in the political and economic spheres. He has an observant eye for detail. The result is a book well worth reading.

FRANK MORAES

Contents

Red
China

An Asian View

Introduction

I spent the winter of 1958-1959 in People's China and traveled extensively—by plane, train, car, and jeep—visiting a dozen major cities, a few villages, and four communes. I went as far as Harbin in old Manchuria in the northeast (the former Manchukuo of the Japanese), Lanchow in the west, the gateway to central Asia, Shanghai, in the east, and, of course, Canton and Shum Chun (through which I entered China) in the south. I had visited the mainland of China once before rather briefly and somewhat unexpectedly during the winter of 1940 as a young student on my way to the United States for study. Though I had passed through Hong Kong several times in the years that followed, this was my second visit to the mainland.

My aim in visiting China was to study within the time at my disposal the numerous economic, social, and cultural changes that the Communists have been able to bring about in less than a decade. My interests covered, in general, China's universities, colleges, and schools, hospitals and clinics, factories and plants, agriculture, industries, and, in particular, her population problem and policies, together with her now-suspended family planning program.

After returning to India, I wrote a series of articles on my impressions for *The Statesman* of Calcutta and New Delhi and the *Illustrated Weekly of India* of Bombay. The former series was syndicated outside India by the Associated Press and has appeared in a few hundred newspapers. Parts of this book have also been printed in *The New York Times Magazine, The Reporter,* and *Contemporary China.* I am grateful to the editors of these publications for permission to utilize these articles here.

3

I went to China with no prejudices or political passions, opposed though I am to Communism on the basis of both the outmoded nature of its economic theory and its denial of democracy and freedom. Since I am a social scientist in my native India and not a politician, I have not identified myself with any political camp for or against Communism in India or elsewhere. But this does not mean that I have no preferences in political and economic institutions. I believe in and have an abiding faith in democracy and the parliamentary, representative form of government in the Western liberal tradition which we are trying to evolve in India—political freedom for all peoples, no matter what their level of cultural evolution; an expanding economy in which both public and private enterprise can play useful roles; and an economic system in which present economic inequalities can be reduced to a minimum.

As such, I am, like most of us in India, opposed to imperialism and colonialism, to totalitarianism of both the right and the left, and to economic and social institutions that deny the average citizen food and freedom. (This simple credo, by which I suppose most of us live, was later to be characterized by my Chinese hosts in our discussions with the terms "bourgeois," "capitalistic," and "reactionary.")

Therefore, I went to China with an open mind to observe and evaluate impartially, but not to take the sample sights of a guided tour as universally valid. While I must record here my gratitude to my numerous Communist hosts in China, who extended uniform hospitality and kindness to me, answered most of my questions while firmly disagreeing with my views on the anachronistic nature of Marxist economic reasoning in the atomic world, and arranged almost all the things I wanted to do in China, I must also confess that I went to China curious, excited, and ready to be impressed, but that I came back sad, stifled, and disenchanted.

When peace came with the defeat of Japan in 1945, China found herself in possession of a far-flung realm, including

Japan's old Manchuria and Taiwan and other islands. Here was a splendid chance to establish democratic political institutions (China, of course, had never known real democracy even under the Kuomintang regime), rebuild her war-devastated economy, and rehabilitate the lives of her long-suffering millions. America was ready to help with men and materials to heal China's war wounds and to act as an honest broker to restore peace between the Kuomintang and the Communists. But the old Chinese leaders were found miserably wanting. They went back to their favorite pastime of amassing personal fortunes. The man in the street was betrayed. It was no wonder that the KMT fell like ninepins and that Mao and his peasant army took over China from Peking to Shanghai, from Chungking to Nanking, without in most places firing so much as a single shot. The people felt relieved. Here was something untried but promising; peace, unknown in the lifetime of most Chinese, had arrived.

But I am afraid the Communist peace of the last ten years, despite tremendous material progress, has turned out to be the peace of a graveyard. What has happened in China during these ten years? What have Mao and his men done to China?

As I look back now, I am unable to lay my finger on the exact reason for my disappointment. I stayed in the best hotels, the only hotels where foreigners can stay, had the best of Chinese and European food, and received most hospitable treatment. (Mr. Nehru's friendly foreign policy toward all had apparently impressed the Chinese, and, at the time of my visit, they affirmed their lasting friendship for India. Subsequent events have shown how sincere these affirmations of the Chinese really were!) I traveled extensively and in comfort. Many people put themselves out to supply me with obscure facts and figures in the unexplored realm of Chinese demography. And yet I did not make a single friend to whom I would care to write a personal letter; everything was impersonal and mechanical.

I have visited many countries in the world and invariably have found people to whom I was attracted by virtue of common interests and ideals and by that inexplicable something which draws people together. I have stayed in their homes, and I have continued to enjoy their friendship through correspondence. But in China I did not find a single person who talked freely to me as man to man, and all the courtesies that were extended to me resulted from the directives of the people in power.

I was surprised to find that modesty is not one of the Communist virtues. Even the most highly educated Chinese, whom I had known in America or Europe, played the same monotonous official record which described China's expanding economy with staggering statistics of production. After a week of meeting officials and professors, I found I could almost guess what the next person was going to say, for it would be the same song, merely sung from a different platform.

Above all, I sensed that I was never really alone and that some unseen eyes were watching me, apart from those of the official interpreter who traveled with me all the time that I was in China. Maybe it was a false fear—I do not know. But the moment I crossed the little bridge at Lo Wu by foot and entered the train on the British Leased Territory bound for Kowloon on my return journey, I regained my lost sense of freedom. I am unable to explain the psychological reason for this relief beyond merely recording it.

There are countless aspects to the Communist experiment in contemporary China, all of which deserve serious attention for many reasons. In India, China is our neighbor and, in addition to a 2,000-mile rugged frontier, we have at some points a direct and accessible common boundary. Not only have the Chinese certain historic cultural traits in common with us, but their political history during the last century has not been entirely unlike ours. Though nominally sovereign, they have suffered from a semi-colonial status from the First Opium War of 1840, involving unequal treaties with Western powers, autonomous concessions and settlements, treaty ports, railway zones, spheres of influence, leased territories, and extraterritorial rights, up until the Communist "Liberation" in 1949.

China occupies an area almost equal to all Europe, and her people number today nearly 700,000,000, or about a quarter of the world's population. And, last but not least, she embarked upon an experiment which seeks to accomplish in one day what other nations normally take twenty years to do. This, in fact, is a Chinese Communist slogan: "Twenty years compressed into one day!"

What is this Communism they are after and how are they trying to achieve it? Is Chinese Communism the same Communism we know in the Soviet Union, or is it different in any material particulars? It is true that the pattern of economic organization in any country is its own affair, and, from one point of view, none of our business, especially since we are wedded to a policy of coexistence. But I believe it is very important for us to know what it is with which we are coexisting.

II

Even the most casual traveler in Red China cannot but be especially struck by certain aspects of the people and their economy that are highlighted by the present regime.

The first is dress: for almost everyone—men and women of all ages—is dressed in blue trousers and a buttoned-up high-collared coat like Chairman Mao's. (At least 95 per cent of the people wear this blue uniform.) To a newcomer, men and women look almost alike, for all the women have taken to short bobs (shoulder-length or shorter). It was explained to me that the women's new haircut, replacing the twin or single pigtail, saves time in combing and washing;

and I must agree that this new hair-style needs no attention. Obviously a woman need only run a comb through her hair and she is all set. Hundreds of thousands of men and women in blue padded pants and coats, and with soiled shoes (it is "bourgeois" to shine one's shoes, I was told), look like an endless army of blue ants scurrying on their appointed tasks. (The term "blue ants" has been used so often to describe the Chinese Communist masses that it is becoming overworked. But I cannot think of any other phrase which so aptly describes the blue-clad millions of Communist China.)

This dull uniformity numbs one's vision at the beginning, but one soon grows used to seeing a whole nation in blue uniform. Yet what is important is that this blue uniform is only an external symbol or manifestation of an inner regimentation of the people's life and thought.

The second thing that no one can escape is the ubiquitous loudspeaker. I first heard it at the frontier station of Shum Chun when I boarded the train which was to take me to Canton. The radio haunted all my waking and many of my sleeping hours till I left the same frontier station on my way out of China some weeks later. The voice blares away at one in the bus, in the train, in the tram, in Pullman sleepers and dining cars, on street corners, in villages, towns, and cities—just about everywhere. Even in the most backward and traditional villages I saw the loudspeakers hidden in treetops. One can escape the sun and moon—but not the loudspeaker.

And what does the radio pour out day and night? The answer: everything that the government approves and wants to convey to the citizen. It is the most important mass medium for the official "news"—news of the nation's progress, the industrial output, instructions on how to make a native smelter, how to defeat the American "imperialist" and the Chiang clique, how to be a good Communist, how to be neat, how to denounce the rightist, how to cook sweet potatoes, where not to spit, and a thousand other things, interspersed with the traditional Chinese opera, with its deafening gongs and cymbals, as well as martial music and marching songs. A few times on the Pullman, I had to feign illness so that I could remove the plug under the loud-speaker in order to enjoy a few hours of quiet. The citizen does not have a minute of silence in which to rest his mind or reflect on his new life.

The reason behind the loudspeaker is really a simple one. In a far-flung nation of 700,000,000, where literacy is not widespread and where the printed word is consequently relatively ineffective, the only way to reach the citizen is via the radio and the relaying loudspeaker which cannot be controlled and cannot even be turned off. I once heard on a train journey a three-hour non-stop speech of the chairman of the Chinese Communist Youth League who was speaking from Peking. The subject: "How to Be a Loyal Communist."

The third aspect of the country and the people that greets one forcibly is the extraordinary cleanliness and neatness. Public health and sanitation are attended to with positive vigor. There are practically no flies, no rats, no dogs, and no sparrows in China. (The destruction of sparrows was not to improve public health but to save grain, which the sparrows would otherwise eat.) People no longer spit anywhere they like. The streets, the pavements, the curbs, and the sidewalks are all swept clean, and they stay clean, morning, noon, and evening. I did not see a single Chinese throw a banana skin or a cigarette butt on the floor or pavement. One sees many people going about with white cotton masks covering their mouths and noses because they might sneeze and spread their cold germs. Neat traditional-style privies had been put up in most of the villages that I visited. And on only two occasions did I see a fly—once in a dining car when the waiter promptly brought a fly-swatter and made effective use of it.

At an exhibition in Harbin, I was shown by a peasant a little invention called a "rat detector." It resembles a stethoscope, with a small amplifying motor mechanism in the middle and a long, tapering antenna. You put the "stethoscope" into your ears and place the ends into the suspected rathole, and you can hear the slightest noise of the remotest rat. And once you thus locate the rat, you can, of course, easily kill it.

And how are the streets and sidewalks kept clean? Apart from the regular methods employed by other countries of providing an efficient sanitary staff and appealing to the civic conscience of the people, China uses the free and patriotic services of children between the ages of eight and seventeen. These youngsters, called "Young Pioneers," wearing red scarves (the Communist version of Boy Scouts and Girl Guides), stand on the pavement morning and evening and shout through cardboard megaphones, "Don't spit! Don't spit!," in a monotonous chorus. I saw on one occasion, in a crowded market street in Peking, an old man spit on the pavement. A Young Pioneer, from apparently nowhere, immediately rushed to him, took him by the arm, and asked him, "Comrade, what will Chairman Mao say when he hears that you spat?" The old man, who had been unconscious of the act, offered profuse apologies and disappeared into the crowd, promising better behavior worthy of a comrade in the future. I am sure he will never again spit in public.

This does not mean that everything is spick-and-span or that the rural and urban areas are models of sparkling cleanliness as in a Swiss or Scandinavian community. Canton, for instance, looks like one vast Calcutta slum, but the dingy old buildings and the cobbled streets onto which they abut have been swept clean. The dreary scene has become orderly.

The fourth aspect of the Chinese scene that cannot escape one is that the whole nation is at work, hard at work, twenty-four hours around the clock. Three shifts in a textile mill or steel plant or a drug factory may be required for technical reasons. But, in China, people do everything on a day-and-night basis. I was told about this by my Chinese friends but did not believe it. It was brought home to me one late night (at 1:00 a.m.) when I was being driven home to the Peking Hotel, where I was staying, after a many-course dinner with some Chinese officials. I saw the roads lit for miles on both sides by thousands of electric lights strung like festoons in a fairyland. It looked as though countless three-ring circuses were giving their performances. My guide explained that these lights meant that people were working. Doubting that people could be working that late, I stopped the car at random and inquired. It was true. About a thousand workers were building the new Peking Opera House so that it might be ready for the tenth anniversary of the Revolution. The work had been going on night and day on a three-shift basis. This Opera House will, when completed, house some 8,000 people; the stage will rise, revolve, and sink, and the acoustics will be perfect; and neither the free nor the Communist world will have seen a structure like this anywhere.

It was the same story with buildings in other cities. In one suburb of Peking alone, where a new cultural center is being created, I counted some eighteen massive structures rising, being built day and night. They will house various technological research institutes that will carry on research in coal, steel, petroleum, and water conservancy—and these institutes are usually completed in three or four months.

I have visited many parts of the world, in Asia, Europe, and the Americas, but nowhere have I seen men and women from teen age to old age work so hard day and night. I have quoted the Chinese slogan that twenty years' work must be accomplished in one day. This is the basis for the hard work that the Chinese are putting in on all their reconstruction, and one hears that every project has been completed before the scheduled date; everything is "leaping forward."

This twenty-four-hour round of work is not confined to any particular pressing sector of the economy; it embraces practically every field of economic endeavor; whether it is making a road or building a bridge, harnessing a river or housing a colony, producing steel or fabricating textiles, it is the same story.

Not only do they work all the time, but they do so in such massive numbers. One sees twenty people pulling a loaded cart—some pulling with ropes like animals and some pushing from behind. One would expect in a "people's democracy" that people would not be substituted for animals. But I have seen men and women even pulling a plow! The reason for this unhappy phenomenon is that people are at the beck and call of the regime, and they need not be paid high wages. So the economy can afford to waste human labor, which in terms of dignity and monetary value means nothing because people are expendable. What could be accomplished by two men is to be done by twenty. A hundred people toil on one acre of land, and literally thousands work to put up a building on a shift basis. And yet, paradoxically enough, everyone from the minister and department head down to the Intourist guide will tell you seriously that China is underpopulated and that there is an acute labor shortage.

Whether or not one likes the means adopted, "the People's" China has determined to catch up with the advanced world. And here they maintain that they have "surpassed" Great Britain in various sectors of the economy and that they hope to overtake even the United States in a few years. But there is no way of testing the validity of these claims.

Another aspect of the Chinese scene which impresses the visitor is the new status of women in China. Of course, in this as in many other aspects, the Communists did not start with nothing. A certain degree of emancipation had been achieved before they took over. Yet to a large extent, the role of the Chinese woman was confined to the bearing and rearing of numerous children. A Chinese wife catered to the needs of her husband while her youth lasted; and when she became old or unattractive, he took a concubine as easily as he bought new clothes. And in times of famine, it was the infant girl or the young daughter that was sold to the landlord or those who ran the houses of ill fame.

But this picture has been greatly altered. The Chinese woman has become the equal of man with a vengeance—legally, politically, morally. The double standard of morality has gone, and male chauvinism has disappeared. There is no prostitution any more. The Chinese woman is no longer So-and-So's wife but a worker in her own right. She works hard and long hours like any man, and her wages are paid to her. She is no longer under the supervision of her father, husband, and son. There is no job that is not open to her. I have seen many a woman at skilled work in steel mills, textile factories, heavy-tool plants; she drives a huge lathe, wields a two-ton hammer, controls traffic in big cities, runs cultural centers, and sometimes holds down a job far away from her husband in the interest of national production. She can obtain an abortion or a divorce without too much bother, and she can and does denounce her husband at Party meetings if she suspects him of rightist or bourgeois tendencies.

The Chinese woman's feet, which were first unbound in 1911, have now been unbound in more than a physical sense. She has finally come into her own. And this is all very good. But, on the other hand, she has ceased to be feminine. She uses no cosmetics, and not the least bit of jewelry adorns her. She is correct and proper everywhere she goes and in everything she does. She is disciplined, regimented, and made to work for the glorification of the State. Millions of women are on the march—going somewhere, or returning from work, grim and serious, earnest and purposeful—all in

padded blue uniform with nothing to distinguish them from
the men, with no smile for anyone, no, not even for the all-
embracing State.

Yet another striking aspect of the contemporary Chinese
scene is the country-wide political propaganda concerning
who China's friends and enemies are. At present, the whole
nation has been taught that there is one great socialist friend
of China—the "selfless" Soviet Union—and one irreconcilable,
"imperialist" enemy—the United States of America. The
friend is understandable, for 90 per cent of the heavy
machinery, an overwhelming majority of all technical experts, and almost all the blueprints of China's industrial
progress are from the U.S.S.R. The Russians have special,
preferential treatment all over China. They are now, in fact,
building special new hotels for Russians so that they can
have their own life without meeting or mingling with any
other foreigners from within or without the Communist
world.

Besides Chinese, the only other language officially recognized in China is Russian. From menus to theater notices,
from directions at stations and airports to travel information, we find only two languages: Chinese and Russian.
Russian is taught in most universities. I have seen students
using Russian textbooks in medical colleges and technological universities, and Soviet books have taken the place
of American books in college and university libraries. In
every factory I visited, I was told the same story of the
"selfless help" of the Soviet Union in giving technical assistance and machinery. Whether it is the Heavy Machine
Tool Factory in Harbin or the Iron and Steel Corporation at
Wuhan or the great new bridge on the Yangtze river linking
the north and the south of China with the triple cities at
Wuhan—all have been accomplished with Soviet technical
help. The Russians draw up the plans, bring the machinery,
and raise the plants with, of course, the help of Chinese

engineers and workers. But the Soviet engineers stay behind the scenes, and one sees only the Chinese manning the machines and directing the factories.

Russian literature, Russian ballet, Russian teachings, and Russian thinking have invaded China from Mukden to Canton. China is fast becoming an image of Russia. It is no wonder that the Chinese have erected massive structures in honor of Sino-Soviet cooperation and friendship, and these buildings usually house permanent exhibitions of the technological achievements of the Soviet Union—which are extremely impressive. The Communists have gone about this business of the Russianization of China in a thorough fashion.

On the other hand, there is the painful contrast of China's attitude to America. America has acquired a permanent adjective—"imperialistic"—in the Chinese language. Today, everyone from the village schoolgirl to the cadre in the communes and all the way up to the cabinet minister will tell you that China's Number One Enemy is the United States. In every town the visitor is greeted at the station or the market place or the busy thoroughfare by huge posters —some forty by sixty feet—depicting (in 1959) Communist China crushing America and her then Secretary of State, John Foster Dulles. The most common posters were of three kinds. One showed molten iron pouring out of the mainland of China onto Dulles and Chiang on the fast-sinking island of Taiwan. The second type showed the American G.I., in his uniform and steel helmet, being pierced to death by a Chinese soldier's bayonet. The third showed Chiang and Dulles hanging from a Chinese noose. All available mass media have been harnessed to din into the Chinese that America is the greatest menace to peace and prosperity in China. And I believe they have largely succeeded in training a nation of 700,000,000 to hate another country— a country which, despite her self-acknowledged failings, has done more than any other to promote free political institutions in the world and which tries very hard to practice what she preaches.

Various campuses that had been established and sponsored by American institutions have been renamed, and their U.S.-educated Chinese faculties have been de-Americanized. One can see films and exhibits of American interference, espionage, and other subversive activities on the mainland, though the exhibition of American germ warfare is now closed. After going around the Tsinghua University—now renamed the Peking Technological University—I asked whether this was the campus that had been run with the United States Boxer Indemnity Fund. I was told that only a measly few thousand dollars had been spent on that campus by the Americans in the past, but that it was just as well, for Tsinghua has trained only lackeys of American imperialism.

They have also closed down the Peking Union Medical College—donated and run by the Rockefeller Foundation for a number of years. This institution, by all accounts, had rendered valuable service to the people, but it had to be wound up to erase the memory of its past connection with America. When I visited it, the college was no longer in existence, but the hospital had grown and continued to minister to the sick. The Peking Union Medical College has now become the Chinese Medical Academy of Sciences—a post-graduate research institute.

But what is China's case against America? It is a simple one. America should withdraw her Seventh Fleet and get out of Taiwan so that China can occupy it. The Taiwan issue to them is purely a domestic problem in which no foreigner should interfere. "Taiwan is an internal problem. It is an extension of our civil war, if you like. We know how to deal with Chiang. We may liquidate him for his past criminal acts or appoint him a governor. But the Americans are in the way." This, I think, sums up correctly their attitude. Their second grievance is that the United States is preventing China from taking her rightful place in the United Nations. And here they made appreciative and grateful references to the efforts of the Indian Prime Minister and Krishna Menon to get them their legitimate seat in the United Nations. (This was, of course, before the Tibetan uprising and the Chinese raids on India's frontiers. Today, oddly enough, "friendly India" has become "expansionist India.") These twin grievances stem from the basic one of America's non-recognition of China. "Is Communism the barrier?" they ask. Then how is it that America has recognized the Soviet Union and Poland?

It is obvious that all this ignores numerous historical factors which account for the two Chinas—Nationalist and Communist—today. And even more basic is the question of recognition of regimes which come to power through force and bloodshed.

Whatever the merits of the Sino-American dispute, it is a sad commentary, to say the least, on Communist China's tactics that they should seek to promote internal unity by whipping up hatred against America—a country which has no territorial ambitions, opposed though she is to the Communist ideology. However, the psychological need for creating this anti-American hysteria is obvious from the Communist point of view. The creation of an external enemy who threatens to destroy the very existence of China is a powerful force to cement internal unity and promote the prestige of a regime which is less than popular with its 700,000,000 people. It is odd that one does not hear as much about British possession of Hong Kong, Kowloon and the New Leased Territory, nor of Portugal's Macao. Maybe the time is not ripe enough to brand them officially as "imperialists" and to agitate against them on a national scale.

This anti-American tirade left me rather cold. It is doubtful whether anyone in India even at the height of Mahatma Gandhi's Civil Disobedience Movement felt as anti-British as the Chinese are today anti-American. During India's long fight for freedom, the people's righteous indignation was directed against something vague and impersonal called "British imperialism" and not against Britons, singly or collectively. Maybe the comparison is not valid, or perhaps this is begging the question, for Mao does not pretend to be a non-violent Mahatma. And yet, though it sounds trite, the *means* are of supreme importance. How different is India's approach to international problems even today in comparison with China's! The Indians have had a running dispute with Pakistan for fourteen years, and, whatever the world might say, we Indians are more sinned against than sinning. And yet India is far too civilized to launch any crude, anti-Pakistan propaganda offensive on a national scale. Right now, as I write, even in India's border dispute with China, the country is behaving with admirable restraint —perhaps too much restraint!

The last aspect of the Chinese scene that becomes apparent even to the most casual observer is their honesty in internal affairs (false production statistics aside), which is in striking contrast to their blatant dishonesty in international relations. By this, I do not mean the elimination of corruption in government, though that also has been attended to. I mean the honesty of the average citizen. On the second day after my arrival in Peking, as I stepped out of the hotel, my guide and interpreter exclaimed: "Look at that 'no-man counter,' and nothing is stolen!" I looked, but did not grasp at first what he was driving at; but it dawned on me a few moments later. It was a little kiosk where some newspapers and journals were stacked beside a plate to receive the money when the passer-by bought a newspaper. The price of the journal was written on the top. This kind of newspaper sale is common in the West—in London and New York. He continued: "A thing like this was impossible under the Kuomintang, but now the people have become absolutely honest. There is no need to steal, for the government provides everything." A minute later, he asked: "Do you have anything like this in India?" I said that the average citizen of India was certain.y honest but that nobody had started these "manless counters" as far as I knew.

My interpreter was quite correct. People have become absolutely honest, though I am afraid this honesty is more the product of fear of the regime's severe punishment than a change in personal ethics. At every place where I had to pay a bill, I just held out my wallet—the small currency notes have Chinese numbers and it is difficult to know the denomination—and the salesgirl brought back the correct change. (There was no need to check the change.) It had become a matter of national honor. There was no tipping anywhere. Once or twice I forgot about this and left some change on the table in the dining room. The waiter did not call me back, but later I found the change had been placed on the desk in my room. Tipping a comrade worker for doing his duty is not only bourgeois but a positive insult.

The beggars and bandits, thieves and thugs, prostitutes and pickpockets have disappeared. The bandits threw up their arms and vanished when they realized that the Communists meant business. The beggars, once so ubiquitous, have also disappeared. I consider this a major achievement for an underdeveloped Asian country when it is remembered that beggars have not completely disappeared in Italy or Spain and that they exist in some disguised, if dignified, form even in England. In all my travels, I came across a beggar only once, and that was in Hangchow—the beautiful city of the West Lake. My two guides became extremely concerned at the sight of the beggar and went off to get the police. They profusely apologized to me as though the beggar had harmed me, and they kept repeating that he was a criminal who had escaped from a labor gang. It is true there is no need to beg, for the government is certainly willing to give you a bowl of rice and put you to work. In most countries, beggars, apart from the physically disabled, resort to begging not because they cannot find some work but because they are constitutionally indolent. In China, there are no longer any indolent persons, for indolence is simply not tolerated.

I

1

Agriculture in China

What have the Communists done about China's insoluble hunger? While there were some shortages of grains, edible oils, and fats, and even quasi-famine conditions in certain regions about three years ago, the Communists have seemingly tried hard to solve the food problems from the quantitative point of view. Apparently no one is really starving in China today. At any rate, no one seems to be dying of starvation. There is no rich food for the masses (the situation is different for the Communist leaders); there is neither variety nor anything more than bare sufficiency. But the age-old problem of diners without appetites at one end of the city and appetites without dinners at the other no longer seems so obvious. Many, in fact millions, have died under the Communist regime in China, though not of starvation. The common man does not have meat or fruit or anything remotely like the abundant and delicious food we visitors receive in hotels and at banquets in China. But everybody seems to get at least a bowl of rice and some cabbage. And this is saying a great deal when it is remembered that the population of China today is about 700,000,000.

Any satisfactory solution of the food problem in Asian countries implies revolutionary changes in land-ownership on the one hand and methods of cultivation on the other. The Chinese Communists have effected, by and large successfully, such drastic changes. (We shall for the moment ignore the terrific human cost involved.)

The Communist agrarian reforms have passed through four distinct stages from 1949 to 1959. I do not think these stages were necessarily planned as such for a ten-year period. The government embarked on them as circumstances demanded and as the political climate permitted. Of course, the over-all objective of food for all workers and some kind of collective ownership of land was there from the very beginning, though the earlier foreign (particularly Indian) observers were misled on the real and revolutionary nature of the Chinese agrarian program of land distribution. (There were some who were even more basically misled into the belief that the Chinese Communists were not really Communists at all, but merely agrarian reformers!)

The first stage of the land reform movement witnessed the public trials of the landlords. When the long-suffering peasantry realized that the new regime meant business, they accused the landlords of all the crimes known to man, from harsh treatment, withholding grain from a starving peasant's family, raping the peasant's daughter, or taking his women as concubines, down to brutal murder. We know that many landlords were guilty of some of these crimes, but, when they were accused by the peasants at this time, they had no lawyers to defend them, nor was any code of law or ethics followed. Communist justice is summary and of a different kind. Most, if not all, landlords pleaded guilty for the simple reason that they knew their end was near, no matter what their defense, if indeed they had any defense. It is officially estimated that about 3,000,000 landlords were executed, but according to external observers the number executed was closer to 20,000,000. Now the land was available.

The second stage involved the distribution of land to the landless peasants. On June 30, 1950, the great Agrarian Reform Law, that veritable Magna Charta of Chinese agriculture, came into force. The major objective of this law was not so much to raise the living standards of China's impoverished peasantry as to facilitate the transition of the Chinese economy to collectivization and industrialization. Commenting on this proposed Agrarian Reform Law, Liu

Shao-chi, the Party's theoretician and pamphleteer, and now head of the State, observed on June 14, 1950:

> The basic reasons for and the aim of agrarian reform are different from the view that agrarian reform is only designed to relieve the poor people. The Communist Party has always been fighting for the interests of the laboring poor, but the viewpoints of Communists have always been different from those of the philanthropists. The results of agrarian reform are beneficial to the impoverished laboring peasants, helping them partly solve their problem of poverty. But the basic aim of agrarian reform is not purely one of relieving the impoverished peasants. It is designed to set free the rural productive forces from the shackles of the feudal land-ownership system of the landlord class in order to develop agricultural production and thus pave the way for New China's industrialization.

Thus, according to this law, "the land-ownership system of feudal exploitation by the landlord class shall be abolished, and the system of peasant land-ownership shall be introduced in order to set free the rural productive forces, develop agricultural production," and thus pave the way for New China's industrialization.

This was the reform for which the Chinese peasants, generation after generation, had waited for some 4,000 years. Now, at last, this permanent charter of agrarian reform had come to liberate the peasant from the yoke of the landlord. Communists and their sympathizers the world over, who knew of the promises of the Chinese Communist agrarian reformers, heaved a sigh of relief. "Ah, we knew the Communists would keep their promises and give land to the landless tillers. Did we not say that Mao and his men were simple peasants at heart whose passion in life is nothing more than agrarian reform and meting out justice to the long-suffering, land-hungry peasants?"

A very complex machinery was set in motion to distribute land to the landless peasants on the basis of numerous criteria, the most important of which were, of course, political affiliation and sympathies, and poverty. The average peasant received a few *mou* of land (one *mou* is equal to a sixth of an acre). There was understandable jubilation among some 500,000,000 peasants. But unfortunately it did not last long.

Within two years, the third stage was launched. It was a campaign to prove that private ownership of land was neither socialism nor Communism, and that it was both a serious economic barrier to greater production, which was so desperately needed, and a theoretical obstacle to socialist reconstruction. It is true that the peasants now had the land, but they were "helped to discover" that this was not an economic proposition and that collective and large-scale cultivation alone could solve the problem of China's agrarian poverty and eternal hunger. Thus collectivization was ushered in.

This program of collectivization was an unexpected blow only to the ignorant peasants, but not to those who knew the mind of the Chinese Communist leaders. For, as early as 1943, when Mao was still in the wilderness of the Yenan Caves, he had obviously made up his mind on the question of collectivization, for he then pointed out in a speech:

> As for the peasant masses, a system of individual economy has prevailed among them for thousands of years under which a family or a household constitutes a separate productive unit; this scattered, individual form of production has been the economic foundation of feudal rule and poverty. The only way to change this state of affairs is by gradual collectivization, and the only way to bring about collectivization is, according to Lenin, through cooperatives.

The peasants felt cheated, but they were made to see the need for collective ownership, for their plots were tiny —a matter of a few *mou*—and this "pocket-handkerchief farming" was not yielding enough. Intense cultivation, use of abundant fertilizers, eventual mechanization, and over-all better land management were impossible on small plots, and beyond the resources of individual peasant owners. Hence the need for simple cooperatives, which were to be only a prelude to collectivization. From a modest beginning of only 300 agricultural producer cooperatives in 1952, the number rose to 14,000 in 1953 and to 600,000 in 1954. By the spring of 1956, China could boast of 1,300,000 agricul-tural cooperatives. This meant that only a small number of the 500,000,000 peasants were outside the cooperatives. One can only imagine the total regimentation and the vast coercive effort involved in this reorganization when one realizes the robust traditional individualism of the average Chinese farmer. With this collectivization, the State took away the land which it had so ceremoniously distributed to the peasants only a few years earlier.

While all this collective ownership and cooperative farm-ing did increase the yield, China was not yet out of the woods from the point of view of the needed food supply. Her population had been increasing by a net annual addi-tion of 12,000,000 to 15,000,000 during these years, due in some measure to the rigorous public health program which had been adopted all over the country and had resulted in gradually declining death rates.

Hence the fourth and the present stage—"the people's communes"—which were causing such serious heart-search-ing during the last few days that I was in China. The Chi-nese leaders and officials are very proud of this latest de-velopment, for here they have gone one step beyond the Soviet Union. I shall return to the communes later.

II

China's mainland covers an area of some three and a half million square miles (3,657,765). As such, it is the third largest country in the world. The Soviet Union leads the world with 8,597,000 square miles, followed by Canada with 3,843,144 square miles. China is followed by the United States of America with an area of 3,615,210 square miles, almost equivalent to the area of China. The United States of America is followed by Brazil with an area of 3,286,170 square miles.

For a predominantly agricultural and underdeveloped country like China, this huge area appears to be of great potential value, but actually much of the land mass is of little or no use.

The country can be roughly divided into two geographical, natural regions with considerable contrast if an imaginary line can be drawn from Yunnan Province in southwest China to Heilungkiang Province in the northeast. The western region (excluding Tibet and the Chamdo area) would consist of some 40 per cent of total land area but with less than 5 per cent of the country's total population. Here in this region lie the uninhabited deserts and wastes, plateaus and mountain ranges of China.

The eastern region, on the other hand, covers some 58 per cent of the total land area but accounts for about 95 per cent of the total population. The fertile deltas, plains, and river systems have been the source of the sustenance of China's millions through the centuries.

Agricultural development has always been a major problem in China's economy. Floods and droughts have periodically ravaged the country, resulting in famine and epidemics. The country suffered from these devastations with such regularity that, to an alien observer, China became the land of famine. The governments in the past, throughout the country's long, checkered, and turbulent history, had been so helpless in the face of Nature's uncontrolled vagaries that the people became fatalistic and accepted the periodic famines and epidemics with stoic resignation as an inevitable part of the regular scheme of life.

China has been importing grain since 1721. And during the last one hundred years, what with a series of wars with Western nations, the near-continuous Japanese aggression since 1931, a thirty-year civil war aggravated by a six-year World War II, not to speak of the skirmishes of the warlords and the raids of the bandits—China has been in a chronic state of political unrest, economic dislocation, and recurring famine. China as a nation has not known real peace for even a decade during the last one hundred years. It is amazing that land and agriculture were not in a worse plight than they were in 1949 when the Communists gained political control over the mainland.

About a quarter of a century ago, when China, in the throes of a severe and widespread famine, appealed to the International Red Cross for relief, they declined to help on the ground that the International Red Cross was designed to meet national *emergencies,* but that famine in China was not an emergency but a chronic state of affairs! This cynical attitude was, of course, based essentially on facts, but the verdict rankled in the minds of those Chinese who gave thought to such matters.

The food situation between the termination of World War II in 1945-1946 and the fall of the Kuomintang government in 1949 was incredible. It was so desperate that the price of a measure of rice, thanks to skyrocketing inflation, was many thousands of *yuan*—ironically enough, the Nationalist *gold yuan!** Prices spiraled upward, not from month to month or even week to week but from hour to hour. This inflation alone, according to some students of Chinese

---

* Today, a *yuan* has the same purchasing power as a rupee—about twenty U.S. cents. But the official exchange rate is fixed at forty-one cents per *yuan* or 2.4 to the dollar.

affairs, hastened the downfall of Chiang Kai-shek and his
government.

III

In Peking, I met some officials of the Ministry of Agriculture, and also had discussions with Mr. Chen Sien, Director
of the Bureau of Long-Term Economic Planning of the
National Planning Commission. He talked to me at length
about China's rapid agricultural advancement. He readily
reeled off astronomical and incredible figures on the progress
that China had made during the last nine hectic years of
the Communist regime.

"For a long time China's problem has been the problem
of food," he told me. "We have suffered in the past from
so many famines that the external world usually associates
our country with famine. But now all that is a thing of the
past. We are using new methods of cultivation and we have
brought more and more land under cultivation. Today, the
area of land under irrigation is some 60 per cent of the
total area of cultivated land, whereas under the Kuomintang
it was about 20 per cent. The amount of organic fertilizers
used for each *mou* is about ten tons per year, and we are
not making use of any chemical fertilizers. Peasants are
using what I may call indigenous or organic fertilizers made
from night soil, river mud, compost, and horse and cow dung,
and this manure has given us a 60 per cent increase in yield."
(His figures on the use of organic fertilizers seemed fantastic,
but he had still more statistics to give.) "Secondly, we are
using better seeds. An additional 2,000,000 *mou* of land
have been put under cultivation since the new regime came
into power, and, using these better seeds, our 1958 yield
was double the figure for 1957."

Talking to me about cotton, he claimed that, in 1958, the
United States of America produced about 2,626,000 tons,
whereas "China had produced 1,000,000 tons more." "I
mean long staple cotton," he added. "And all this tremen-

dous increase has been accomplished without any mechanization. Production has become so great that we have to revise our old concepts of agricultural production. Land can perform miracles when we bring modern science to bear on land management.

"China, of course, is still economically backward, but this backwardness was caused by imperialism and feudalism and not by too many people. China's feudalism prevented greater production, and hence living standards were miserably low; but since Liberation our living standards have been considerably raised. The wages of workers increased by 42 per cent during the first Five-Year Plan and the income of the average peasant has increased by 30 per cent.

"The struggle between Man and Nature is a long one, of course, but today, with the development of technology, Man can better Nature. As far as China is concerned, we are rich in natural resources. We have large tracts of land, and there is wide space to explore, colonize, and settle. China is densely inhabited only in the coastal regions, while in the border regions the population is very sparse. Now we have only to mobilize people, move them to these sparse areas, settle them there, and let them fight against Nature." He outlined to me plans for future development of China's agriculture, all the while reeling off further astronomical production figures. (Most of the figures, unfortunately, do not seem to make much sense.)

"The real reason behind our incredible output of grain is our land reform. During the upsurge of the land reform, 700,000,000 *mou* of land were distributed to some 300,000,000 poor and farmless peasants. Of course, the average was only two or more *mou* per head, but even this was better than nothing. This agrarian reform brought about a major change in the countryside. Once upon a time, i.e., ten years ago, the villages were overpopulated, and, at the slightest sign of famine or pestilence, there was a tremendous rural exodus —people leaving their homes and going to the cities in search of work and food. But there was no employment in the cities, and the peasants became beggars, thrown on the charity of the few rich people. But now the picture has completely changed. We now have, believe it or not, a labor shortage on the farms because we have found it useful to use large numbers of people to work each plot of land." I interrupted the Director here to say that I had seen men pulling plows in some parts of China, and I asked him why men were being used for this purpose instead of animals. He told me that animals were being reared, by and large, for food and not labor, and he gave me a brief lecture on the dignity of labor.

Then he went on: "As we have no mechanization, we need all the human labor we can get for deep plowing and close planting. And, because of the land reform, our peasants are full of enthusiasm to increase production. The government, of course, extended various kinds of help to them, such as agricultural loans, better seeds, farm implements, and technical advice.

"But now the land reform is over, of course, and we are concentrating on further increasing production under such new patterns of ownership as collectivization and communes.

"We are now engaged in a Leap Forward Campaign in both agriculture and industry. As a result of the Great Leap Forward, the output of cotton and grain doubled in 1958 compared to 1957. In 1949, the output of grain per capita was 400 catties." At the end of our talk, the Director repeated the current, well-publicized slogan that "there is no low-yield land—only low-yield thinking. Once the marriage between land and technology is effected, the law of diminishing returns will become a bourgeois banality."

In Peking, I also visited the Institute of Agricultural Economic Research. The Director, formerly an officer in the Communist Army, received me cordially and introduced me to his technical staff. The members of his staff were relatively young men and had had advanced training in foreign

universities, mostly in the United States, and some of them
had been working under the Kuomintang government in
various capacities. The Director introduced me to the
Technical Director, who gave me the following statistics:*
"Our total agricultural land is 14,300,000,000 *mou* and
the cultivated area is about 1,900,000,000 *mou*. There are
1,500,000,000 *mou* of virgin and barren land which have
yet to be reclaimed for cultivation and habitation. Actually,
the whole country has not yet been properly surveyed, and
when such a survey is undertaken, as we are planning, we
shall probably realize that we have more land than we can
make use of.

"Take, for instance, our forests. The land under forest is
1,500,000,000 *mou*, but in the past the Chiang Kai-shek
clique never developed the country's forest resources. It is
estimated that our forest products alone will give us enough
resources to mechanize our agriculture."

Mr. Wang Shao, Deputy Secretary-General of the Chinese
Academy of Agricultural Sciences, was then introduced to
me. Mr. Wang talked to me about animal husbandry. He
said: "In 1949, the animal population of China was very
low. During the war years, most animals were killed and
eaten. There was no proper scientific breeding and to my
knowledge we never had a livestock census. By 1958, the
number of big animals (cows, horses, buffalo, mules, and
camels) numbered some 83,000,000. Sheep and goats alone
numbered some 98,000,000, while in 1958, the pig population
had risen from almost nothing to 190,000,000. Pork is one of
our staples, and we plan to double the production of this
animal." He inquired whether we in India ate pork, and I
answered in the negative. "It is a pity," he said. "We consider pork a delicacy. But in the past, only rich landlords
could afford it. Now, however, even in the most remote

---

* Communist official statistics often contradict each other, even though
they are *official* statistics. Thus it is often impossible to decide which set
of figures is more realistic or nearer the truth.

villages the poor peasant can have pork at least once a day."
(This statement did not agree with what I had seen in
the villages, and it must be remembered that what I was
shown was probably better than average.)

The Director now joined us. Discussing the Great Leap
Forward in agricultural production in 1958, he gave me
the following list of chief aims:

1. Water conservancy.
2. Improvement of the soil through successful soil recla-
mation and better soil management practices.
3. Manufacture of indigenous fertilizers and greater application per *mou* of the same.
4. A better variety of seeds.

"These are all done in other countries," he added, "but we
have now introduced three innovations, i.e., close planting,
deep plowing, and intensive manuring." I asked for an explanation of close planting, and he replied that it simply
meant that more seeds per furrow were used, and that,
with a greater number of seeds per *mou,* so many more
seedlings sprouted, almost all of them growing into sturdy
plants. This meant that, for the same area, a bigger crop
was grown. "We are also experimenting with deep plowing,
which means that instead of the traditional depth of a few
inches, we are now plowing anywhere from two to four
feet." The Director added that, although lots of people pooh-
poohed this idea and said it was a waste of labor, they had
already found that deep plowing gave them tremendous
yields.

"And last, the agricultural plan for the future embraces
the entire countryside," he concluded. "Once we modernize
and mechanize our agriculture, we shall have rationalized
food production and saved land. We cultivate today some
250,000,000 acres of land. But, according to our plans for

the future, we shall devote a third of these acres to cultivation of grains and raise on them more food than we are producing on the entire acreage at present under cultivation; a third will lie fallow; and a third will be used for flowering plants, fruit trees, and grass. We shall make our countryside as green and beautiful as England."

Though I was bothered about the means that would be adopted to bring this about, I must confess I was touched by this grand vision of removing poverty and ugliness from China's countryside.

"When were you last in England?" I asked.

"I have never been outside China. But I have seen pictures of the English countryside. Have you been to England?" he wanted to know. I told him that I had and gave him my impression of Britain's beautiful countryside. He nodded his head and said, "Yes, yes. That is what China will be like soon."

Agricultural production is indeed rising, though one cannot swallow without a grain of salt the astronomical figures of production that the officials reel off. The methods adopted to achieve the Great Leap Forward in agricultural production are: 1.) all cultivable land (except in uneasy Tibet) has been brought under the plow; 2.) constant irrigation (I was shown on one farm an experiment of irrigation with hot water. My guide told me that hot water quickened germination and growth. I don't know whether this is scientific or not); 3.) deep plowing—two to five feet deep (on another experimental farm they are plowing by detonating a series of small bombs placed under the ground); 4.) close planting (more seeds per furrow); and 5.) adding enormous amounts of manure to the soil—night soil, green leaves, river mud, compost, bone ash, and bacteria—layer after layer interspersed with good earth.

China seems to be approaching a solution to the problem of food supply for her teeming millions, but it is difficult to check the figures of her agricultural production. It is possible that they are generalizing from success on small experimental farms. It is possible that their bookkeeping is faulty, or it may be that China's ancient soil has also joined the Communist Party's Great Leap Forward Campaign. It is anybody's guess.

2
The Communes

The setting up of the communes is the fourth and present stage of China's agricultural revolution. As we have already pointed out, when the Communists came to power in 1949, Mao Tse-tung promised the Chinese peasants that he would eliminate the landlords and restore the land to the tillers. This promise was carried out between 1950 and 1952, and the landlord class was liquidated, either being killed or permitted to reform themselves by working as landless peasants in remote areas. Thus the former landlords were left in an even worse position than those once-landless workers who now received some land.

The second stage of the revolution was ushered in on December 16, 1953, when the Chinese Communist Party passed a resolution entitled "On the Development of Agricultural Producers' Cooperatives" and accordingly set up such simple cooperatives all over the countryside. By the end of 1954, i.e., within a year, some 400,000 basic and elementary cooperatives, embracing some 15,000,000 households, had been set up.

Two years later, on June 30, 1956, the third stage of the agricultural revolution, involving the collectivization of agriculture, was introduced. On that date the Communist Party issued a set of "Model Regulations for Advanced [as opposed to simple and elementary] Agricultural Producers' Cooperatives" by which the peasants joining the cooperatives were directed to give up their privately owned land and other privately owned major means of production, such as farm animals and implements, to the collective ownership of the advanced cooperative. The peasants were permitted to keep poultry, small animals, and other domestic goods.

And in August, 1958, came the fourth and perhaps final stage of the revolution—the all-embracing communes. The Politburo of the Chinese Communist Party, at a conference held at the end of August, 1958, adopted a resolution on "The Establishment of the People's Communes in the Rural Areas." The major objective of the commune was announced as "the over-all and continuous Leap Forward in agricultural production in the whole country and the growing elevation of the political consciousness of the 500,000,000 peasants." According to this resolution, the communes had developed as "the logical result of the march of events."

According to the Communist officials, the setting up of the communes was the most momentous and exciting advancement in Chinese agricultural and over-all economic development, for here China had gone "one step beyond the Soviet Union." The communes were springing up everywhere, all over the countryside, spontaneously, and, if you can believe the officials, the peasants were begging and pleading with the cadres to let them organize themselves into communes! No sheep ever went more happily or willingly to the slaughter house than did the Chinese peasants who begged to be organized into communes! They were beginning to catch on even in urban areas. Chairman Mao, a high-placed official told me in Peking, wanted to organize even Peking, the nation's capital, into one big happy commune—the first metropolitan commune in the world.

II

What is a commune? In essence, it is the merging of a number of collective farms and villages into a single organizational and administrative unit which is responsible for the all-round development of agriculture, forestry, animal husbandry, and fishery, as well as of industry. The peasant (agriculture), the worker (industry), the trader (exchange), the student (culture and education), and the militia (military affairs) are brought under one single, unified command.

A commune, to begin with, should not embrace more than 2,000 peasant households to enable it "to explore the practical road of transition to Communism." At the early stages, the development of the communes was not to be rushed and was supposed to be a "voluntary" affair. For the time being, such methods as nominal payment for work are to continue until the idea "from each according to his ability and to each according to his needs" is achieved. The "people's commune," I was told, is the best form of organization for the attainment of socialism and the gradual transition to Communism.

The idea of the commune is, of course, not really new, for, shortly after the Russian Revolution in the years 1918-1923, it was tried out in the Soviet Union on a small scale.

The attempt was an idealistic experiment to abolish all private property and to own everything in common. The members were to work according to their ability and to receive according to their needs. But the experiment failed for various reasons, among which the Russian peasant's deep-rooted attachment to his farm as well as the regime's unwillingness to back this particular experiment with force were perhaps the major ones. Thus discredited, they were abandoned, never to be resurrected again. The Soviet Union eventually evolved the *kolkhozy*, where both private property and collective ownership coexist.

The Chinese have not read Russian history in vain, and they are aware of the incredible difficulties that Russia experienced in collectivizing her peasants. Winston Churchill records in *The Hinge of Fate* a conversation he had with Stalin in 1944 concerning collectivization in the Soviet Union:

> "Tell me," I asked, "have the stresses of this war been as bad to you personally as carrying through the policy of the collective farms?"

This subject immediately aroused the Marshal. "Oh no," he said, "the collective farm policy was a terrible struggle."

"I thought you would have found it bad," I said, "because you were not dealing with a few score thousands of aristocrats or big land-owners, but with millions of small men."

"Ten millions," he said, holding up his hands. "It was fearful. Four years it lasted."

The Chinese peasant's love for his private plot of land is no less intense than the Russian's. But, as we have seen, the Chinese Communist leaders "eased" the unsuspecting peasantry into the communes by gradual stages, and, with the bloodbath involving the landlords in the countryside behind them, it is unlikely that the emasculated peasants, now well drugged with propaganda, will rise against the communes.

History is repeating itself. And China is indeed going one step beyond the Soviet Union in herding her peasants into the communes.

III

What are the aims and functions of the communes? The over-all aim of the communes is a thorough overhaul and reorganization of the entire social, economic, and cultural fabric of Chinese society. It is the ultimate in public ownership.

The commune is not concerned merely with carrying on agriculture and industry on communal lines. Its major aim is to revolutionize the bourgeois and feudal conception of all human relations: between parents and children, husband and wife, man and man. The commune is designed to transform the Chinese way of life beyond all recognition, completely tearing it away from its ancient moorings of familial loyalty and solidarity.

Such drastic and fundamental changes are possible only when the traditional role of women in Chinese society is completely uprooted and reorganized. According to Communist theory, labor is the source of all value, and the labor of women, half of China's working population, must be tapped and harnessed for production in the new Communist State. To achieve this, domestic life is being reorganized, and women are being made to forsake their traditional roles of homemakers. They can no longer be primarily wives and mothers, tending the kitchens and raising families, for each wife and mother cooking and taking care of her immediate family involves a tremendous waste of labor. If one wife can cook for a hundred families, ninety-nine wives can be released for more productive labor. Both the answer and the logic behind it are simple. Collectivize or rather Communize the home, and a tremendous amount of woman-power is released which can be placed at the disposal of the State. Loyalty is transferred from the narrow biological or joint family to that larger, all-embracing, and demanding family —the State. By the end of 1958, some 90,000,000 women from about 100,000,000 peasant households had been relieved of their age-old domestic duties in Honan and Hunan, Shantung and Shansi, Kiangsi and Liaoning, to work for the State.

Secondly, the communes are to provide the much-needed capital for China's planned large-scale and rapid industrialization. Today, the level of living of China's teeming millions in terms of the basic requisites of civilized existence is low, lower than that of other areas in Asia like Japan, India, and Ceylon. Her vast and mounting population is a drag on China's efforts at over-all economic development. The increase in national output, particularly in agriculture, effected through heartbreaking Stakhanovite methods, is swallowed up by the sizable net annual additions to the population, leaving no perceptible rise in the people's level of living. That is, every increase in production is used up in current consumption, leaving no significant margin of savings for effective investment to make quick, heavy industrialization possible. In a word, China is running very fast to stand still.

How is this shortage of much-needed capital resources to be overcome? "Since the establishment of the people's communes, the percentage of income each commune must allocate to the reserve fund has been greatly increased, and the portion distributed among members has been radically cut. In 1956, the Communist regime stipulated that 70 per cent of the total agricultural income should be distributed among the peasants; in 1957, the income received by the peasants as compensation for labor still reached 53.2 per cent of the total agricultural income. Since the establishment of the people's communes, however, local expenditure represents on the average only 30 per cent of the total income, and the other 70 per cent goes to savings and investment."

The third task of the communes is to convert the peasants into a working class. Peasants all over the world are conservative and offer resistance to radical reform, and the Chinese peasants are no exception. As Lenin pointed out long ago, "Peasants constitute the last bourgeois class," and their transformation into a proletariat is one of the urgent aims of the Chinese revolution. Peasants must be educated to give up their bourgeois individuality and their love for their land. The communes, by collectivizing everything the peasants ever owned and paying them a wage (to begin with), convert them into agricultural workers. And once the peasants, the backbone of China's cultural continuity and tradition, have been eliminated as a group, the Communist revolution will really be on its way.

Such drastic changes are possible only when the problem is attacked on military lines, and here is the fourth aim of the communes. The "people's communes" are administrative and functional units where "labor is organized along military lines and things are done the way battle duties are carried out, and the people live collectively." Every member of the commune becomes a soldier, literally and metaphorically. The commune becomes a labor battalion.

An editorial appearing in the *People's Daily* (the official organ of the Chinese Communist Party) dated September 4, 1958, pointed out: "In the communes, everyone should become a soldier. Young men eligible by age and all demobilized service men should be organized into militia, put under constant military training, and required to shoulder the mission assigned by the State."

This does not simply mean that all able-bodied adults in the communes get some military training. While military training is given to men and women in the communes, the slogan "Act as if in battle" implies that normal work on farms and in factories is to be carried out along military lines.

If the peasants and workers become in an effective sense industrial armies, production can be stepped up. Life becomes tense, and work under "tense" conditions can increase efficiency and production. The *People's Daily* of October 20, 1958, points out a new motivation in Communist China. It says: "Tension is the feature of the order of life in our present era. If we do not live tensely, how can we free ourselves from the burden of poverty and backwardness left to us by history? And how can we build socialism and enter the Communist paradise?" I wondered if the word "tension" had been wrongly translated. But when I asked a high Communist official in Peking about it, he assured me that tension was the correct word. If China is to catch up with Britain in fifteen years, peasants and workers cannot afford to relax and lead quiet lives. The certain way to increase production is to make people work under strain and stress. And the only way to keep the workers in a state of both physical and mental strain is to make them "Act as if in battle."

This embattled life to increase production involves shock labor tactics. What is shock labor? It is an exaggerated form

of Stakhanovism, with neither time nor production limits.
Whether it is production or construction, the battalion works
incessantly, night and day, perhaps days on end, without
rest or relaxation. Its simple aim is to obtain maximum results by massive, non-stop attack. Reason: to battle poverty.
Means: a life of physical and mental poverty!

A life of fatigue and tension all the year round for all the
peasants and workers in every commune for a period of
fifteen years so that China's production can beat Britain's.
What more can a totalitarian state ask of its slave subjects?

IV

Of the four communes I visited in November and December, 1958, the one north of Peking and only a few miles
from the city was in the throes of being set up, the next two
in Shansi were being reorganized, and the fourth one, in
Chi-li-ying, north of Chengchow in Honan, had been completely organized and had been running a few months when
I arrived.

In the commune a few miles north of Peking there was no
spectacular progress to report, even by the ardent and
voluble Director who took me around. "One of the most important changes contemplated is to transform our housing,"
he said. "You have seen the peasants' huts, the small, un-
comfortable houses scattered all over the villages without
plan or purpose. But when this commune gets going, all
these huts will be pulled down. In fact, we have already
started demolishing them. And we shall have a few huge
buildings of flats. In fact, eventually one skyscraper in this
village will house all the villagers from this and all the
neighboring villages when they are brought under this commune. In a few years our countryside will be dotted with
self-contained skyscrapers with their own kitchens, dining
halls, tailoring establishments, schools, gymnasiums, etc."

He paused to let this vision of the skyscraper-studded communes of the Chinese countryside-to-be sink into me.

"They tell me you have visited America often. Do they have skyscrapers in their villages?" he asked. "No," I replied. "I have no doubt we shall surpass them in this matter," he asserted with complete confidence.

I was interested to learn that this commune-in-the-making is planning to have, like other communes, its own militia. The reasons behind this plan to militarize the communes were not made clear to me, though I raised the question with the directors of the different communes I visited as well as with my otherwise well-informed interpreter. As I went around the farms, I saw a few bundles of rifles standing here and there on the fields. I saw groups of farmers drilling on lines of military formation with old-fashioned rifles. I inquired how far the peasants had advanced in learning to fight with live ammunition. The Director didn't answer my question, but pointed out that the great commune movement was in its *first* stage and I had come just when the whole country was becoming commune-conscious and the fever was catching on.

"Please come again after a year, in 1960, and we shall show you the finished product!"

V

The Chi-li-ying people's commune is located about eighty miles north of Chengchow in Honan Province. From Chengchow we reached Hsin-hsiang by train, and from there we drove in a jeep along a dusty road beside a canal to the village where the headquarters of the Chi-li-ying commune was located. As we approached Chi-li-ying, I noticed that the mud road had been swept clean and watered so that no dust rose. The Director met us at the entrance to the village and welcomed me in a neat little speech. I now forget how many visitors I was told there had been before me, but the

road was worn smooth by the many foreign delegations as
well as groups of visitors from other parts of China who had
come to see and learn from Chi-li-ying.

Of the four communes I had visited, Chi-li-ying was the
best organized from the official point of view. It was a model
commune, a kind of showpiece, and it appeared to control
every conceivable aspect of human life from morning to
night, from birth to death.

I spent a day in this commune, and the Director, a former
landless farmhand, drove me around and showed me everything. This commune was to set the pattern for the whole
country and was organized in the upsurge of the Great Leap
Forward in agriculture.

The Director told me that Chairman Mao happened to
visit this area in 1958 to see the agricultural cooperatives.
All the peasants met him and entreated him to let them have
real Communism. They complained that the agricultural
cooperatives did not go far enough and that the cadres
(officials) were lukewarm. Mao agreed with the peasants
on the need for real communal ownership and pointed out
that the peasants were more progressive than their cadres.
He suggested the setting up of a commune. And, lo and
behold, the next day—July 20, 1958—the Chi-li-ying people's
commune came into being! It was one of the earliest communes to be set up in Honan Province.

Apart from the enthusiasm of the peasants, why was this
commune really set up? The Director explained that, with the
advent of the Great Leap Forward in agriculture, new and
difficult problems in agricultural organization had cropped
up which could not be dealt with even by the advanced
agricultural collectives. They had already become old-
fashioned.

The second reason for the commune, according to the
Director, was the need for industries in rural areas. It was
discovered that, without industry, increased agricultural output was impossible. The area produced a lot of cotton and,

in the past, it had to be transported to a distant city where the ginning plant was located; the seeds had to be sent elsewhere for extraction of oil, and the cakes for fertilizer had to be produced in the city. If the raw materials could be converted into manufactured goods as far as possible in the rural areas where they are grown, the difficult question of transportation, the bottleneck of present-day China, could be eliminated. Not cottage industries, but regular, large-scale industries for the rural areas were envisaged. But industries demand capital, skilled labor, and technical knowledge which the agricultural cooperatives and collectives could not provide. The only way out, under the circumstances, was the commune.

The third reason behind the commune, the Director pointed out, was the difficulty encountered in paying for work in the cooperatives. "We used a system based on points. Workers who scored the highest number of points in production were paid the highest wages. But we discovered that the point system did not work smoothly, nor was it just. Some workers labored beyond regular hours and others worked during nights. Sometimes they worked singly and sometimes on teams. And it was difficult to calculate the exact remuneration due to the workers. The commune solves all these problems because there is no question of cash payment to its workers."

The Chi-li-ying commune comprises sixty-eight villages composed of 12,133 households with a total population of 57,551 people. The land, the houses, the farm implements, the cattle, the cottage industries, and the kitchen utensils are all owned by the commune. It also owns and runs a few native iron smelters (steel production, at least as far as smelting all scrap iron is concerned, has become a cottage industry), repair plants, wheat flour mills, tailors' establishments, brick and tile kilns, fertilizer plants, etc. It manages 228 public canteens where all adults eat their daily three meals in hostel-type mess halls.

There are 135 creches where babies—from a week to four years old—are taken care of. There are 130 kindergartens where children four to six years old are housed and taught. There are two coeducational middle schools—equivalent to our high schools—where 1,450 students between seven and sixteen years of age are receiving some instruction on the basis of the new syllabus drawn up by the commune and approved by Peking. Besides these, there are thirty-six Red and Expert Schools (Communist professional technical or trade schools) where bright and Communist-biased youngsters of both sexes are taught various trades. Attached to all these schools are hostels in which the children live.

The commune also runs two large rural hospitals with fourteen outpatient departments which administer traditional Chinese medicine (like herbal remedies and acupuncture).

The adult population is distributed over 146 production teams to work on rice, vegetables, and cotton fields, small industries, creches, kindergartens, canteens, schools, hospitals, tailoring houses, repair shops, etc. The families are broken up, with the children separated from the parents and sometimes even husbands and wives separated from one another. To suit the all-demanding objective of increased production, husbands and wives may have to work on different and scattered production teams.

All the homes in the villages constituting Chi-li-ying are owned by the commune, and there is not an empty room, for all couples and single men and women are distributed over the total available rooms. The little children are, of course, in creches and kindergartens, the older ones in the middle schools, and the old people in the "Happy Homes for the Aged." Thus, thanks to the people's commune and collective ownership of all available space, the rural housing problem has been solved.

I visited three creches and kindergartens, all on the same street and housed in the better type of rural homes. We were expected, and the moment we arrived we were greeted by charming, chubby children in their padded clothes shouting "Ni hau, Bo-bo! [How do you do, Uncle!]" and clapping their hands. They looked happy, carefree, and contented. The woman teacher moved to a small piano in the corner and began to play. The children automatically formed a ring and began to sing the now-familiar songs, "Socialism Is Good!," "Communes Are Good!," and "Chairman Mao Is Our Savior!"

"Do they go home to their parents?" I inquired of the teacher.

"Not normally."

"Don't the children miss their parents?"

"I don't think so, because we provide for all their needs. They have necessities and even comforts here, comforts they would never have had in their own homes, in the past I mean," replied the teacher. We were then led to a room where an odd assortment of commune-made toys was neatly piled in the corner. The teacher explained the daily schedule that the children followed and, pointing out the toys to me, said with satisfaction that the children not only had food and clothing and medical care but toys and games as well.

As I took leave of them, I wondered whether the children missed their parents or not. I couldn't tell. Maybe the teachers gave them the affection, love, and security they needed. I hoped so.

I visited two of the twenty-four "Happy Homes for the Aged." They were housed in the former landlords' homes. The old folks were roughly in the over-sixty age group. They clapped on our arrival, and the elder of the home took me to the table in the living room—obviously the dining place—and offered me a handful of shelled peanuts. He told me that in the past, that is before Liberation, their lot had been a sad one. They had been dependent on the unpredictable charity and hospitality of their sons or relatives. Before Chairman Mao had set up the "Happy Homes," either they had to labor in their advanced age to earn their meager subsistence or they were made to feel like drones and parasites.

Was this true? It sounded rather off-key to me, for no country in the world had a greater reputation for honoring and caring for its aged than China. As the old man's words were being translated for me, I had the feeling even more strongly than usual that what was being said was "inspired."

An old lady who still hobbled on her bound feet, the first one of her type I was to meet in the countryside, led me gently to her room and proudly displayed the new woolen blanket on her *k'ang* (built-in bed), the first one she had had in many years. For the first time in her life, she was really being cared for, she said. She had a roof over her head, sufficient food, and a warm bed. All thanks to Chairman Mao.

The old folks did not go to the other canteens where the adult workers ate their meals, but ate in their own "homes." I was told they hated to be idle and that, since they were anxious to work, they had been given light tasks to do—spinning and weaving and feeding the chickens.

What is a working day like in this commune? Men and women wake up in the morning to the blare of the loud-speakers in the streets. After half an hour of exercise in the open air—there is tremendous emphasis on physical fitness—they go off to the canteens for a communal breakfast. Then they break up to form different production teams based on individual ability and aptitude for work. Husbands and wives, parents and grown-up children are not necessarily on the same team. The teams go off to their allotted tasks in the fields or factories. They reassemble at noon at the various canteens for a simple lunch of rice, cabbage, and sweet potato, and occasionally a little pork. After lunch, they march off to their appointed tasks again. Lunch is taken out to those who work in distant fields so that they can eat on the spot and not waste time getting to and from the canteen.

The food in the commune canteen was of the poorest kind.

Communal cooking cannot have the taste of home cooking. And a peasant youth was permitted to complain, in Peking's *China Youth Daily* dated November 4, 1958, as follows:

> At the sound of the cease-work bell,
> We enter the mess hall to eat.
> Taking one mouthful of rice,
> We find sand between our teeth;
> Helping ourselves to the vegetable,
> We find grass stalks in it.
> We lay down the chopsticks,
> And go to work again.

In the evenings, all have regular classes where they listen to the radio which pours out the latest editorial from Peking's *People's Daily,* the latest production figures in agriculture and industry, how many tons of steel the street-corner furnaces turned out yesterday, the latest measures adopted by the People's Government to liquidate "American imperialism" and the "Chiang clique" on Taiwan, how China has surpassed Great Britain in the production of various industrial goods and, last but not least, the Peking opera, which is now not only entertaining but strangely didactic. Then there is perhaps a patriotic movie or a revolutionary play or a plain acrobatic show.

And last is the Party meeting which every worker attends, the crowning end of a full day. Here the matchless art of self-criticism is practiced, and the meeting is like some strange mixture of Ku Klux Klan bigots, M.R.A. confessors, and Stakhanovite champions. People rise and confess their drawbacks and failings from trifles to matters of life and death; they criticize their colleagues and upbraid their comrades; and everyone swears allegiance to Big Brother Mao and vows to liquidate the American imperialists, counter-revolutionaries, and other enemies of the people; they promise to increase production if only to regain Taiwan.

Thereafter, everyone retires for the compulsory eight hours of sleep.

I was told that nursing mothers and mothers of ailing children can visit the creches or kindergartens, though the visit to a sick child may be discouraged, for the children are under the care of trained nurses in addition to their competent teachers. Parents must give up their bourgeois emotional attachments, stop worrying about children, and concentrate on work.

This commune which I have briefly described is popularly called "The Commune of the Sixteen Guarantees." Everyone (according to age and sex) is given sixteen guarantees. They are: 1.) Food; 2.) Clothing: each member of the commune is given eighteen *yuan* for clothing, and the amount is adjusted for children. Members can receive cash or clothing, whichever they prefer. The color of the cloth and the kind of dress conform to the national uniform. But clothing is still a problem because of the cold climate and the need for padding it since heating is poor or absent; 3.) Housing: the commune owns all the houses in the area and keeps them in good repair. The commune also has a guest house for visiting relatives and friends of the members of the commune; 4.) Transportation: free transportation from residence to place of work is provided. If a member goes out of the commune on official business, his travel fare is paid by the commune. He is also granted a per diem allowance of one *yuan;* 5.) Maternity benefits: expectant mothers are given forty-five days' leave for confinements and one catty of red sugar which is a must for expectant mothers in rural China. Should the mother or infant need extra or special care due to any complications, they may be sent to the big, modern hospital in the nearest city at the expense of the commune; 6.) Sick leave and free medical aid for everyone; 7.) Free old-age care: old and disabled people do not have to work; but those who want to do so are given some light work; 8.) Free funeral and burial: funeral services are held only for distinguished commune members. No service is held for ordinary citizens. The Director of the commune told me that they would like to replace burial with cremation, but the people are prejudiced in favor of traditional burial, so they are now adopting what the Director called "deep burial." The body is buried at least ten feet deep so that they can use the land —which might otherwise be a graveyard—for orchards; 9.) Free education; 10.) Free upbringing of children; 11.) Free recreation; 12.) A small marriage grant on the eve of one's wedding. When a young couple marry, the bride and groom are given five *yuan* each, that is if both are members of the commune. If a commune member marries an outsider, only the commune member receives five *yuan*. The commune gives a free reception and dinner in honor of the couple; 13.) Twelve free haircuts per year; 14.) Twenty free bath tickets per year (hot water baths); 15.) Free tailoring: making of the blue boiler suit as well as repairing it, and other odds and ends of tailoring; 16.) Free lighting: if a household is provided with electricity, it is free. Where there is no electricity, each couple is given one *yuan* per year for oil for their lamps.

After reciting these benefits—a kind of cradle-to-grave insurance scheme in return for unquestioning, life-long, hard labor—the Director asked me, "What more can one want?"

"Nothing!" I confessed, overwhelmed. "But can one obtain a packet of cigarettes, for instance?" I am afraid I temporarily bogged down under so much material well-being and, at that moment, I could think of nothing more profound to ask!

"We have not overlooked that," the Director responded happily. "Though we have abolished the need for money in this commune, we have provided certain incentives to enable a person to earn one to five *yuan* per month." (At the official rate, this means from about forty cents to two dollars.) That is, if any worker shows tremendous ability or ingenuity or perfects a new technique, he may be rewarded with from one to five *yuan* per month. "This is a kind of bonus," added the Director, "though no one has yet earned this amount."

VI

This is the commune, where human beings are reduced to the level of the inmates of a zoo. But there is a difference. The animals in the zoo do not have to work, much less work hard, and, what is more, they do not have to listen to the blaring and tiring quasi-compulsory radio. The lack of quiet and peace in the countryside, the complete lack of privacy or solitude in which one can retire and reflect, are, to me, more terrifying than all the conceivable hells put together.

Mao had hoped that the whole nation would become one vast, happy commune within a few years, but there seemed to be some bourgeois doubts and reluctance among the leaders themselves. Time alone can tell what the future has in store for China and for the millions cribbed, cabined, and confined in her communes.

When I returned to Peking, some Communist pundits pointed out to me that these communes will develop into the basic social units of the Communist society-in-the-making. "Of course, the emergence of Communism will take a number of years. When the communes increase the total social product and raise the Communist consciousness and people's morality to a higher degree, the differences between town and country, mental and manual labor, and one man and another, will gradually vanish. And last, the State's only function will be to protect the country from external aggression, and, as it will have no role to play internally, it will wither away."

"How much of the State in the Soviet Union has withered away in the last forty years?" I inquired. I received no reply.

The truth is that Marxist theory is all wrong. The State in the Soviet Union, the Mother of Communism, not only shows no signs of withering away, but has on the contrary become the most tightly organized totalitarianism, justifying Lenin's dictum that "force and hatred are the twin functions of Soviet power." But here in Peking a few Chinese Communists seriously assured me that the communes are a prerequisite to the withering away of the over-centralized, monolithic Chinese State. It is difficult to decide whether these Communists are self-hypnotized idealists or deliberate liars.

Less than a dozen years ago, George Orwell, in his novel *1984*, conjured up an incredible, but what now looks like a prophetic, vision of the ultimate totalitarian state. He wrote: "In our world there will be no emotions except fear, rage, triumph, and self-abasement. Everything else we shall destroy—everything. Already . . . no one dares trust a wife or a child or a friend any longer. But in the future there will be no wives and no friends. Children will be taken from their mothers at birth as one takes eggs from a hen. . . . There will be no loyalty except loyalty to the Party. There will be no love except the love of Big Brother."

Can anyone describe the Chinese communes better?

3

China's Industrialization

"Industrialization is the key to our economic advancement and the weapon with which we shall defeat the American imperialists," said the Director of China's Export Commodities Exhibition in Canton with some animation, after presenting me with numerous finely printed brochures and leaflets describing all the industrial and other goods that People's China today manufactures and exports.

"In the past we were industrially one of the most backward nations in the world, thanks to the greed of the imperialist nations and the lack of interest of the Chiang clique. Now you have seen for yourself our exhibits. These are not merely for show. Within less than ten years of the Liberation, thanks to Chairman Mao, we have been able to produce goods which were beyond the dream of all past Chinese governments."

It appeared to be true. I had spent the entire forenoon after an early breakfast going around the wide variety of agricultural, industrial, and other exhibits at China's Export Commodities Fair at Canton, not far from the Ai-chun Hotel on the banks of the Pearl river, where I was staying. A modern six-story building had been put up for the special purpose of housing the exhibition, which had been on for a few weeks. Hundreds of buyers, businessmen, and traders from Communist and non-Communist countries had been visiting the fair to sample and test the goods that China was producing and order them if possible. Several businessmen from countries which had not recognized People's China had been given special visas just to travel to Canton to visit this exhibition. The commodities exhibited could be ordered through Chinese government agencies or certain joint enterprises (a combination of private and State ownership).

I was particularly interested in the exhibition of machinery and modern industrial goods. These ranged from bicycles and wheelbarrows to cars, trucks, and buses, textile machinery, radio and television sets, gramophones and hi-fi's! There were electric stoves, frigidaires, various kinds of laboratory apparatus and precision instruments and, last but not least, locomotives! This was indeed an impressive array of manufactures for a country that had been notoriously backward and underdeveloped until a decade ago.

Was it possible that China had manufactured all this in less than ten years—that she had changed from a feudal, agrarian economy, and one that was a shambles on the eve of the Communist usurpation of political power, to an industrialized economy able to produce these goods? I raised this question with a knowledgeable British businessman, an old China hand who had for many years been a prominent resident of Shanghai and who had come to the exhibition from Hong Kong to look it over and find out if he could order some machinery. He said that, though all the exhibits bore the label "Made in People's China," he thought only a few, such as bicycles and wheelbarrows, were really the products of China's factories. And a few others were certainly made in China with Soviet engineering skill, but only in experimental quantities. They were certainly not in use in China, and if any foreign buyer should order even a thousand of any of the exhibited items, China would probably take at least five years to deliver them.

"What about the prices?" I asked.

"They are attractive enough," he conceded. "In fact, lower than Japanese prices. But no foreign firm has tried their machinery, and we don't know how good it really is."

Later in the evening, at the hotel, I learned over tea with a Pakistani industrialist who occupied the room next to mine that some exhibits of modern textile machinery (which ap-

peared to be an improvement over its British counterpart)
were actually imported from the Soviet Union. But the
Chinese had removed the labels indicating the origin of
manufacture and replaced them with "Made in People's
China"! This, of course, shocked me, for I had come away
from the exhibition considerably impressed. But I had no
way of verifying the Pakistani gentleman's statement. However, a Sikh businessman of our party from Hong Kong,
who had been born and bred in Shanghai and spoke both the
Mandarin and Shanghai dialects fluently, agreed with the
Pakistani industrialist.

"I don't know about this particular textile machinery," he
said, "but I am inclined to agree with you. I visited this
exhibition last year and ordered some drugs, but I never
received them. Later on, through certain private channels,
I discovered that the drugs exhibited were of East German
origin but packed in Chinese containers! This exhibition is
put on not so much to do business as to impress foreign
visitors."

Whatever might be the truth in the allegations of these
seasoned businessmen that China has been indulging in
these less-than-honest tactics for propaganda purposes, no
one can seriously deny her tireless effort to industrialize her
economy. She has made an industrial start. She is trying in
every way possible to forge ahead. And it is likely that she
will catch up with India and Japan in another decade.
There is in China a new spirit, an ardent desire, and a grim
determination to become an industrial power. Nowhere is
this to be seen more clearly than in Wuhan.

II

Wuhan, a city of some 2,000,000 inhabitants in the heart
of China on the middle reaches of the Yangtze, has become
symbolic of the new China's determination to industrialize

the nation, revolutionize her transport, and integrate her plans for a centralized and regimented economy.

In the past, Wuhan represented the general confusion and medievalism so characteristic of China. The three cities of Hankow, Hanyang, and Wuchang were separated for centuries by two rivers, the Yangtze and the Han, and there were no bridges to link them together. One could not travel straight through from the south to the north, from Canton to Peking, by train or automobile, for Hankow, Hanyang, and Wuchang came in the way, and, through the ages, the only communication between them was a primitive ferry boat. But now the Communists, with the technical assistance of Soviet engineers, have built a great bridge across the Yangtze river, connecting the three towns and linking the north with the south.

As soon as I arrived in Wuhan, I was taken to see this bridge. I was driven across it, and at the other end we stopped and took a lift down to a hall where the Superintendent of the bridge was ready with a speech, tea, and fruits.

He rapidly recited how the Yangtze is the largest river system in China and how, in Wuhan, the confluence of the Yangtze and its tributary, the Han, has divided Wuhan into three parts, and how the flow of communications, trade, and commerce was interrupted and hindered. The Canton-Peking Railway had to halt here, and one had to take a ferry that could not be used when the river was in flood, which it was more often than not.

For centuries Chinese emperors had dreamed about a bridge over the Yangtze, but nothing had ever come of it. The Kuomintang twice appropriated huge sums of money to build such a bridge, but, while the money disappeared from the coffers of the State, no bridge materialized. According to the Communists the Kuomintang ministers built villas with the money instead (though actually nobody knows what really happened to the money).

There was another difficulty. It was not easy to build a
bridge across the turbulent Yangtze. Chiang Kai-shek's
American engineers had not been bright enough to devise
a way of doing it.

I interrupted the Superintendent to point out that American engineers had built great bridges in the United States
and other countries and I didn't see why they couldn't have
built this bridge if the Chinese government at that time had
been in favor of it.

"You can blame the Kuomintang if you want to," I said,
"but you surely cannot believe that American engineering
skill, which is responsible for so many marvels in the world,
couldn't build a bridge like this." However, my remarks
provoked no answer.

(The Yangtze bridge is of steel, is some 1,156 meters
in length, and looks something like the Howrah bridge at
Calcutta or the bridge over the Godavari at Rajahmundry.
No one in India gets especially excited over these bridges—
the product of British-Indian engineering skill.)

The Superintendent went on with his speech. The Soviet
engineers took two years to plan this bridge. It was constructed entirely on a new principle called the "colonnade
foundation method," which is purely a Soviet innovation.
This was suggested by a Soviet specialist, and the advantages of it lie in the fact that it is relatively free from the
controlling factor of flood-water level and free from the
effects of seasonal fluctuation, enabling work to be carried
on throughout the year. Compared with the time required
if the pneumatic caisson method were used, the construction
period was shortened by almost two years. As all the work
was carried out above water, the health of the workers was
safeguarded.

He went on to tell me that this great steel bridge is a
two-storied structure designed for the conveyance of both
railway and highway traffic. The railway deck, with a double
track, is underneath and the highway deck above is eighteen

meters wide and accommodates six lanes of traffic. There
are sidewalks on each side of both railway and highway
decks. At each end of the bridge is an eight-storied abut-
ment filled with lifts. The basement of the bridge is a
spacious hall where visitors to the bridge can be entertained
by the authorities.

The steel for the bridge came from the Anshan Steel
Works, all the way from northeast China. Part of the steel
frame came from the Soviet Union. The whole project,
concluded the Superintendent, had been completed, like
every other undertaking in People's China, ahead of schedule. In this case, the bridge was thrown open to traffic two
years ahead of schedule.

"I could tell you much more about this great bridge built
by the people for the people, but I learn you are pressed for
time," concluded the Superintendent.

As I rose to leave, the Superintendent told me that through
the centuries spanning the Yangtze river had been but a
dream, and the people, out of their long years of suffering
from neglect and misrule, had made up a ditty about the
Yangtze bridge:

> The waters of the Huang Ho—
> They never can be tamed.
> A bridge across the Yangtze—
> It never will be laid.

But now, thanks to Father Mao, the children of China do
not have to sing this ditty any more. The impossible has been
accomplished.

III

There are three sights of Communist achievement in
Wuhan which it is almost compulsory for every foreign
visitor to see. One is the great steel bridge over the Yangtze,

the second is the Wuhan Heavy Machine Tool Plant, and
the third and perhaps the most impressive is the Wuhan
Iron and Steel Corporation. After seeing the bridge, we
drove to the Heavy Machine Tool Plant, a huge factory
rather neatly laid out. The Deputy Director, an engineer
(the Director, who was a Party man, was away), received
us at the entrance and took us to the reception room, which
looked exactly like all the other reception rooms I had seen
across the length and breadth of China. (I wondered
whether there was any Party dogma about the size of reception rooms, the settees and tables that furnish them, and the
portraits that hang on their walls.)

After the inevitable welcome speech and the equally
inevitable cup of tea, the Deputy Director asked me whether
I would not prefer to hear him speak before going around
the factory. I said that I would.

He told me that the Wuhan Heavy Machine Tool Plant
produces a large variety of machine tools. The construction of the plant started in April, 1956, and was completed
in July, 1958, which was, as usual, one year and a half ahead
of schedule. (I often thought to myself during my travels in
China that, since everything in the country is finished at
least a year or two ahead of schedule, there must be something wrong with their schedules! They obviously under-
estimate the power of Communism. Or maybe the planners
in charge of schedules are bourgeois!)

The plant covers, the Deputy Director said, an area of
500,000 square meters and it houses nine workshops, including the forging shop, the first machine assembling shop,
the second machine assembling shop, the material-preparing
shop, the foundry shop, and the tool-repairing shop.

There were some 2,000 machines in all, half of which were
imported from the Soviet Union and other Communist
countries. There were a planer four meters in width and
three hundred and sixty tons in weight and a vertical lathe
with a bench five meters long, and other heavy machines.

There were some 5,000 workers in the plant, and the average wage was about fifty-six *yuan* a month.

The plant produced vertical lathes, planers, milling machines, horizontal boring machines, gear hobbing machines, and seventy other types of machinery. The plant is capable of producing a 2,000-ton lathe, if the domestic market needed such a lathe.

With his introduction over, the Deputy Director took me around the factory. I was surprised to find many women workers, most of whom looked young, though one cannot be sure of their ages. On inquiry, I learned that the women did as well as, if not better than, their male counterparts.

"There is complete equality between the sexes today in China, as you must have noticed," the Deputy Director told me. "Women are permitted to work in factories and mines on the same terms as men." This freedom, enabling young women to work in dark pits and heavy plants, did not appear to me to be an especially commendable form of feminine emancipation.

As I did not notice a single Russian expert anywhere in the huge factory, I asked the Deputy Director whether there were any Soviet technicians around.

"Only a few are left here now, and they are in the offices," he said. "Once they have trained a few Chinese, their role is over. The Soviet-trained Chinese have now trained all the workers in the factory. This way we have solved the language problem."

The fact that Russians are not to be seen in factories and offices is true not only of Wuhan but of China as a whole. For though I did meet Russians in hotels and theatres, and at art shows and exhibitions, and on trains and planes, I never ran across a single one working in a factory or instructing Chinese workers, much less ordering Chinese about. The Russian technicians were all apparently well behind the scenes, their presence as inconspicuous as their aid was impressive.

The last but not the least important sight of Wuhan is the large and sprawling plant of the Wuhan Iron and Steel Corporation. This corporation runs the rising new steel city of Wukang—a suburb of Wuhan—on the banks of the Yangtze. I spent a day driving around several square miles, visiting the blast furnace which had just gone into production, the ore-dressing plant, the open-hearth furnace plant, the rolling mills, the refractory materials plant, the huge kitchen and canteen, the workers' homes and grounds, and the halls and houses used for the various social services of the workers.

The Director, who accompanied me in a jeep, told me how they have created this stately steel city from almost nothing, thanks to Chairman Mao, the imperishable Chinese Communist Party, and, of course, the unselfish aid, technical and otherwise, of the Soviet Union.

The plant has been designed according to the latest technical achievements of the Soviet ferrous metallurgical industry. The Russian experts had helped in prospecting for resources, in the selection of a plant site, assembling of materials, drawing up of plans, and assembling and training the manpower. The entire plan of the steel town at Wukang was designed by the Leningrad Metallurgical Designing Institute.

This plant is the second largest integrated iron and steel enterprise in China, the first being the Anshan Iron and Steel Corporation started by the Japanese.

At the end of my tour of Wukang, I realized how much Russia had contributed to the beginnings of Chinese industrialization. If the Anshan Iron and Steel plant was the product of Japanese technical knowledge, the Wukang steel city was clearly the product of Russian knowledge and a witness to Russia's impressive technical aid to China.

I visited the Number One blast furnace and watched the hot, lustrous stream of molten iron flowing out. The furnace had just gone into production a few days earlier, and there was still great jubilation in the plant over its successful beginning. The Director reached for a tiny red flag which had on it Mao's picture superimposed on a steel furnace and pinned it on the lapel of my coat.

As we stood watching the molten metal flow by, the Director could not contain himself. He turned to me with a big smile and said: "This will be our answer to the American imperialists on Taiwan!" It was obvious that the Director took a very personal pride in this new steel city. It was but natural that he should do so, for his fate must have depended on his administrative ability to organize the entire project.

Wukang's ore and raw material base consists of eight ferrous and non-metallic mines. The Tayet mines, some miles away, are the first iron ore base. The quality of the ore is of a fairly high order, the average iron content being about 50 per cent. Modern methods of mining are now adopted, and an electric railroad connects the mines with the Wukang plant. A large, modern ore-dressing plant is located right near the Tayet mines. But the 5,000,000 tons of coal consumed annually at Wukang for smelting and power have to come from six provinces—from the far north, east, and central China. Despite the lack of some of the advantages of localization as far as coal is concerned, Wukang seems to be on its way to becoming eventually China's Pittsburgh. Wukang's present production is about 1,500,000 tons of iron per annum, but they hope to increase it to 3,000,000 tons by 1961.

Before I left, we returned to the small and unpretentious office of the Director.

"We started from scratch three years ago, and already the molten iron is flowing out," he told me proudly.

When I asked him what was the secret of Wukang's success, he said there were several reasons. "First, this plant is set up and run by the Party and not so much by the government."

"But doesn't that amount to the same thing?" I asked.

"Not quite," he pointed out. "While the Ministry of Metallurgical Industry in Peking is in over-all control of this plant, it is really the product of the great efforts of the Hupei Provincial and Wuhan City Committee of the Communist Party.

"Secondly," he went on, "the secret behind the rapid and successful completion of this plant is that here we used a whole division of the Liberation Army for purposes of industrial construction. The question of utilizing an army division for purposes of building a steel plant or plowing the land or laying bridges is usually a controversial one. Here in Wukang we have shown how the Liberation Army could change its profession of fighting and become an army of industrial workers. I think the soldiers themselves realize that, without iron and steel, there can't be much of an army or equipment to fight with.

"And thirdly, here we have more or less tried to abolish the division between worker and cadre. It is true there are numerous specialized tasks and different degrees of technical skill. But here in the steel plant, whenever necessary, cadres have joined in physical labor, and workers have participated in administration. The solidarity between the masses and leaders is complete, and the distinction between intellectual and manual labor has been virtually abolished."

"How many regular workers are there in the plant?"

"About 6,000."

"Their wages?"

"The regular workers receive salaries of between fifty and 100 *yuan* a month, depending on their skill. The staff is paid between 100 and 200 *yuan* a month. My own salary is 200 *yuan*," he volunteered.

I noticed the small gap between the salary of the Director of the whole works and the average worker. The ratio of emoluments between the average worker and the Director of the plant in Wuhan was 1 to 2, but in India the ratio is in the neighborhood of 1 to 20. Perhaps this lack of a big gap between the salaries of workers and heads accounted for the greater loyalty of the workers. Anyway, this probably was one of the factors.

As we were leaving, I asked the Director where he had received his steel engineering training.

"I never went to any school, much less to an engineering college," he answered. "All my life I have been a soldier in the Red Eighth Route Army. But I picked up some facts about steel when I was posted here!"

This was the man behind Wukang—the steel city that epitomizes China's struggle to industrialize her economy overnight.

IV

As I drove back to the hotel, I wondered about China's prospects for rapid and large-scale industrialization. There is no doubt that an underdeveloped country like India or China needs to embark on large-scale industrialization, for it is one of the major means of raising the levels of living of the people. This is generally recognized, and every under-developed country has in recent years embarked upon such a policy, which has helped to siphon off the surplus population from overcrowded land and agriculture in the rural areas to factories in urban areas.

What are the prerequisites for large-scale industrialization? Raw materials, capital resources, technological know-how and managerial enterprise, a skilled labor force, and a market for the products of these new industries. Does China possess all or at least some of these factors in sufficient measure to warrant any hopes for heavy and large-scale industries in the near future—i.e., in the next two or three decades?

Some students of the country have contended in the past that China has few mineral resources and, particularly, that she lacked leading metals such as iron, zinc, lead, and copper. But this pessimism might have been based on the fact that China—i.e., the present area of the People's Republic—had never undergone a systematic geological survey. Such surveys are now being undertaken, and during my travels in Manchuria I met at least three teams of Russians, East Germans, and Chinese who had been conducting geological explorations. It is possible that China may discover mineral resources she never dreamed of in the past.

The trinity of raw materials required for a thriving heavy industry is coal, iron, and oil. China is supposed to possess some of the best coal of coking quality in the world. There are deposits in almost every province. Her iron-ore resources are said to be 4,000,000,000 tons, near Anshan, Wuhan, and Fushun. The area of old Manchuria contains considerable quantities of bauxite, magnesite, and oil shale. China has some oil in Szechuan, western Kansu, and north Shensi. Yunnan has some copper. Inner Mongolia has some lead and zinc. It is therefore possible that, while China is not abundantly rich in her minerals, she has enough deposits for her internal needs at an accelerated rate of industrial consumption for at least some decades.

What about capital resources? Many have felt in the past that any serious plan for China's industrialization would demand billions of dollars of external aid. Can Communist China borrow or can she tighten her belt (the savings above her present subsistence level are negligible) or do both? While it is true that China is too poverty-stricken to effect any real savings over current consumption for investment in basic industries, she is trying to do her best to increase agricultural production and effect some savings. But here her rate of population growth is more or less swallowing up her savings and nullifying her attempts to invest in industries. But fortunately the other avenue, that of borrowing, is open to her. And she has borrowed heavily from the Soviet Union. Here again the one rich country, the United States of America, from which she could have borrowed, is closed to her on account of her own belligerency toward America. As she is not a member of the United Nations, the resources of the World Bank and the International Monetary Fund are also closed to her. But Russia cannot possibly underwrite all the money needed to industrialize China. And it should not be forgotten that whatever Russia has given China is not a gift. While Russia and the Communist bloc are willing to supply China with both capital and capital goods, such supply does not arise out of any altruistic motive, but only as an economic proposition within the framework of ideological sympathy. And the supply of capital resources continues to be more difficult than the Chinese Communists had anticipated.

As for the third factor of technological know-how and managerial enterprise, China is woefully deficient. Here again she is totally dependent upon the Soviet Union for engineers, technologists, and various kinds of specialists. While I did meet an occasional East German engineer or a Polish or Czechoslovak expert, it is the Russians who constitute the bulk of foreign experts. There have been some 30,000 Soviet experts in China at any one time during the last ten years. This apparently large number is not really too many when the area and population of China, and more particularly her industrial backwardness and lack of modern technological education, are taken into consideration. The Soviet Union is not only preparing blueprints and putting up plants and training Chinese on the spot to man modern machines, but is also taking some hundreds of Chinese students every year for training in her universities, technological institutes, and factories. A few Chinese are also receiving training in other countries of the Communist bloc.

The traditional Chinese concepts of manual labor and technical education and the ancient modes of building and training are undergoing radical and remarkable changes. The pressure of industrialization is changing both the pace and mode of the Chinese way of life. The tractor will eventually take the place of the primitive plow, just as the adding machine will replace the abacus.

As for labor, China has a huge and ever-expanding reservoir. The age pyramid reveals that China's population, like most of Asia's population, is a young one. And the Communist emancipation of Chinese women means today that women are made to do heavy work in mines and machine tool factories. Although the country's labor force is not a skilled and trained one, this drawback is gradually being rectified. The illiterate and undisciplined peasant masses are being transformed under the compulsion of Communist brainwashing into a skilled, disciplined, and regimented labor force which can work smoothly in coordinated teams in modern factories with machines of precision. The transformation of the individualistic rural peasant with his traditional mores into a modern, urban, industrial worker is not easy in any culture, but here in China, Communism, with its religious fanaticism, dogmatic zeal, and, most important, limitless power, has a tremendous advantage.

While training a large labor force is difficult enough, the creation of a competent managerial class with executive ability, drive, and vision is even more difficult. And the situation in China is made more intractable by the fact that responsible positions in corporations and plants can only be given to avowed Communists. According to Dr. Peter S. H. Tang, "The lack of skilled and competent personnel has extended also to the ranks of management, and, in fact, to all the leading cadres in the industrialization program, and undoubtedly helps account for some of the worst blunders in managing an enterprise under a system of State planning. The process of criticism and self-criticism in the central and local organs of the Party over the past years has revealed innumerable complaints of ideological backwardness, bureaucratic handling of productive matters, and ignorance in administration, accounting, and technology. Perhaps this lack of basic skills has also contributed to the corruption, delay and waste, and simple lack of enthusiasm which have been reported."

And last, does China have a market? China's huge population should assure her of a ready market, but an impoverished population with little or no purchasing power can hardly buy the products of modern industries. The enlargement of the domestic market implies growth in the supply of consumption goods, an adequate network of transport facilities, and a rise in the wage bill. All this will take many years, for today the level of living of the average Chinese is so low that the domestic market can be dismissed as of no consequence as far as industrial and luxury products are concerned. China, therefore, has to nurture her foreign markets, both within and without the Communist bloc.

In the absence of a domestic market, the government is so dependent on the available foreign market that it responds very quickly to anything which shrinks her markets abroad. (And the free world must remember that one of the effective ways of teaching China civilized codes of international behavior is to ban and boycott her products from the foreign market.)

V

In my travels throughout China, I found it extremely difficult to meet the well-known or distinguished Chinese I had known abroad, particularly in the United States of America, England, and France. I knew some of them had left the mainland and escaped the revolution, but many remained behind. It is interesting that some who were abroad when the Communists took over returned to the mainland voluntarily and offered themselves in the service of the new regime. Among these was the well known American-trained economist Dr. Cheng Han-sen, whom I had known in the United States. I was able to meet Dr. Cheng only after following the usual devious routes that one must traverse in order to establish contact with people in Communist countries. He invited me to dine with him at the International Relations Club in Peking. Over dinner, Dr. Cheng had been very enthusiastic about China's plans for rapid and heavy industrialization, which, he was confident, would make People's China one of the most powerful countries in the world. He was talking to me about the need for military power in terms of arms and ammunition, bullets and bombs, tanks and torpedoes, if a country is to mean anything in the modern world.

I asked him whether China should not postpone the building up of a military machine and give priority to consumption goods and to raising the living levels of her impoverished masses.

Dr. Cheng maintained that guns were more important than butter just now for China. "Don't forget that we have a formidable enemy in the United States." I was interested to hear Dr. Cheng take this now-familiar line of approach, for when I knew him in New York he was a great admirer of the United States.

"Don't you think it will be some decades before China can build up a strong enough military machine to face the United States?" I asked.

"I don't think so," he said grimly. "You wait and see."

"Is China planning to be primarily a land power or a sea power? Are you building up a navy?"

"I cannot go into details. But I know what you are driving at. We cannot fight the American navy with our sampans," he said. He would say no more about this, however, and instead proceeded to enlighten me on his country's plans for heavy industrialization.

"I have seen something of it at Anshan, Wuhan, and Harbin," I admitted. "But I don't understand your priorities."

I pointed to the television set facing us in the dining room, which was featuring a quaint dance of a Chinese minority community from Shanghai. I wanted to know the need for television in a country at China's present stage of economic development, when the peasant did not have adequate clothing or food.

"How many television sets have you seen in your travels?" he asked me.

"Very few," I admitted.

"That is so, for I don't think there are more than fifty sets in the entire nation! But we especially wanted television in China for two reasons. First, we wanted the outside world, particularly the Asian countries which do not have it, to know that we *have* television; and, secondly, we wanted the Western world to know that we have the necessary technical knowledge for television."

* * *

The possibilities of China's industrialization, despite all the well-known obstacles, are immense. China may not become a strongly industrialized nation within a few years, but she can become one in a few decades. And if we do not forget the nature of Communism in general and of Chinese Communism in particular, the thought of a strong, industrialized, militarized China, with her millions goose-stepping across the frontiers, is a frightening one. Those who are dedicated to neutralism and coexistence in the larger cause of peace have no choice but to give some sober thought to this picture.

4
Women in New China

In traditional Chinese society, women occupied a low and subservient position, lower even than the position occupied by women in such Asian countries as India and Japan. Confucius, who wrote of gentle manners and good morals, did not plead for woman's equality with man or, for that matter, for any special rights for the fair sex. On the question of women's place in society, he was perhaps as reactionary as Manu, the Hindu law-giver.

To begin with, parents preferred sons to daughters. Indeed, "preferred" is too mild a word to describe the Chinese desire for sons and the disdain for daughters. In times of famine, it was not unusual for poor parents to leave their baby girl on a rubbish heap outside the city to perish, or, in the last century, on the doorstep of some missionary's home, where they knew she would be taken in and cared for. Female infanticide in China had not disappeared even in the early decades of this century. When a baby girl did grow up— and all during her childhood the care she got was inferior to that which her brothers received—she was married off as early as possible. In her husband's household, she was a semi-slave, under the rule of her mother-in-law, until such time as she herself had borne sons and acquired daughters-in-law upon whom she could wreak vicarious vengeance.

Throughout the centuries, arranged marriages were the rule in China as in other parts of Asia. A Chinese girl had no freedom to marry the man of her choice. She was given in marriage to the man her parents chose for her, sometimes a man much older than herself if he was rich and her parents needed money. When a wife became old or unattractive, her husband usually took a concubine—not a secret mistress whom he visited occasionally but one who moved into the home as the new wife. But a wife had no right to divorce her husband on any account.

No jobs or respectable careers of any kind were open to women. Nor had they any property rights. Even as a widow, the Chinese woman had no legal claim to the estate of her deceased husband. She was simply thrown on the care of her sons, which fortunately was usually both considerate and considerable in old Chinese society. (But the traditional society had begun to crack at the beginning of this century, ancient familial responsibilities were shirked, and there was nothing new to take their place.)

Thus the Chinese woman, when young, was under the care and control of her father; when married, under her husband; and when widowed, under her sons. She had, in a word, no independent existence whatever.

Of course, in rich and affluent homes women were loved and cherished in the Chinese way, more like dolls on children's shelves, decorative to the home. They hobbled daintily, if perhaps painfully, on their bound and stunted feet, dressed in brocades and silks, their hair elaborately coiffured, their mission in life to bear as many sons as they could. But for the vast majority of women in China in the middle and lower classes, life was an unending and unrewarding cycle of toil and labor.

After the 1911 Revolution and during the Kuomintang regime, modest reforms were talked about by women like Madam Chiang Kai-shek with her New Life Movement. But there was much more talk than action, and nothing very substantial came of these reforms. Women's modern education had its real beginnings at this time, thanks mainly to the American missionaries, and some girls went to schools and colleges to become teachers and doctors. Western-educated Chinese, as well as concerned Europeans and Americans in China, encouraged these changes as part of

China's renaissance. But the tempo of change was slow and confined to the cities, with the result that the mainstream of China's life was untouched. The overwhelming majority of Chinese women continued in their traditional roles.

This new education wrought some external changes. Both economic pressure and modern convenience led many women to give up their traditional robes. A few took to Western frocks, but the majority clung to the *Cheongsan* in a modified version. Although many Southerners wore loose pajamas and shirts, it was, when the Communists came to power, the *Cheongsan* that was the common apparel of China's women, particularly in the upper classes. It is a tight-fitting dress that reveals all the contours of the body and tapers snugly below the hips so that it would be impossible to walk in one but for the slit on either side of its skirt. Interestingly enough, one judged the degree of a woman's emancipation by the length of her *Cheongsan's* slit! Among the conservative, the slit was only a few inches high, whereas in others it went halfway up to the waist, tantalizingly revealing the upper thigh.

Characteristically enough, the emancipation of women under the Communists began with their apparel. Gone are the *Cheongsans*, with their variety of color and materials, and in their place is the blue boiler suit—blue pants and blue buttoned-up coat, the same for men and for women, from adolescents to the aged. The Communists, with this dull, drab uniform, have at one stroke established national sartorial uniformity, abolished class distinctions, and with them any individuality in the choice of one's apparel. Except for the hair, it is difficult to single out a man from a woman. And now that so many women have given up their traditional long twin pigtails for the bobbed hair approved by Chairman Mao, the apparent distinction between the sexes is even less.

Trousers and coats for women have been common enough in China through the ages—in winter, men changed into the traditional scholar's gown and women into pants—but

why this dull blue for everyone? I raised the question with
a professor at Peking.

"Don't you know," he asked, "that here in China color has
always had a class status? Yellow was for the Emperor, red
for the mandarin, and blue for the masses. Now that we
are a people's democracy, the color of the masses has become
the national color."

II

This external uniformity in dress was only a symbol of
the new equality between the sexes. The Communists have
effected more radical and far-reaching reforms in the status
of Chinese women since they came to power than were
ever dreamed of all through the centuries.

As early as September 29, 1949, the People's Political Con-
sultative Conference adopted the Common Program. Article
Six of the Program reads: "The People's Republic of China
shall abolish the feudal system which holds women in
bondage. Women shall enjoy equal rights with men in
political, economic, cultural, educational, and social life.
Freedom of marriage for men and women shall be put into
effect."

Some seven months later, this intention was carried out
for all practical purposes when the New Marriage Law
was passed on May 1, 1950. This law guarantees complete
equality of the sexes, free choice of marriage partners,
monogamy, equal rights of divorce, and the protection of
unwed mothers as well as of illegitimate children.

Here are a few articles from the Marriage Law which
need no comment:

> Marriage shall be based on the complete willingness
> of the two parties. Neither party shall use compulsion,
> and no third party shall interfere.

The marriage contract shall be made by the parties concerned of the first part, male and female, at their own will.

The age of consent shall be raised from eighteen to twenty for males and from sixteen to eighteen for females.

No man or woman in any of the following instances shall be allowed to marry: a.) where the man and woman are lineal relatives by blood, or b.) where the man and woman are brother and sister born of the same parents, or c.) where the man and woman are half-brother and half-sister.

The question of prohibiting marriage between collateral relations by blood within the fifth degree of relationship is to be determined by custom.

Husband and wife are companions in a common life and are equal in status in the home.

Husband and wife are in duty bound to love, respect, and assist and look after each other, to live in harmony, to labor for production, to care for the children, and to strive jointly for the welfare of the family and the building up of a new society.

Both husband and wife shall have the right to use either of their family names, his or hers.

Children born out of wedlock shall enjoy the same rights as children born in lawful wedlock. No person shall be allowed to harm or discriminate against children born out of wedlock.

Divorce shall be granted when husband and wife both desire it. In the event of either husband or wife insisting on divorce (unilaterally), it may be granted only when consistent and friendly mediation . . . has failed to effect a reconciliation.

> In cases where divorce is desired by both husband and wife, both parties shall register with the sub-district People's Government to obtain divorce certificates. . . . After establishing that divorce is desired by both parties . . . the divorce certificates shall be issued without delay.

However, two conditions for restriction are provided to protect the wife who is with child and the soldier who is absent on duty for a long time.

> The husband shall not apply for divorce when his wife is with child. . . . In the case of a woman applying for a divorce, this restriction does not apply.

> The consent of a member of the revolutionary army on active service who maintains correspondence with his family must first be obtained before his wife can apply for divorce.

And last,

> Persons violating this Law shall be punished in accordance with law. In cases where interference with the freedom of marriage has caused death or injury of persons with whom interference is made, the person guilty of such interference shall bear criminal responsibility before the law.

This Act has been enforced in most parts of the country with different degrees of severity. As there is neither written civil law nor criminal law in the People's Republic, the nature of the punishment has been left to the People's Judges in People's Courts. The only injunctions were the various ordinances issued by the Liberation Army for its own administration and discipline.

A revolutionary institutional change cannot be carried out overnight. The passing of a law does not necessarily ensure its country-wide adoption, and there was opposition in some quarters, particularly in the rural areas, and oddly enough sometimes from the women themselves.

Though there was a nation-wide campaign to educate the people on the implications of this new marriage law, there was a great deal of agony and heartache in implementing it. The courts were inundated with applications for divorce. Wives who had suffered long as daughters-in-law finally found the courage to come to the courts. Whatever the outcome of their appeal, there were strain and tension, misunderstanding and mutual recrimination between husbands and wives, mothers-in-law and daughters-in-law, parents and grown-up sons and daughters awaiting marriage. There were separations and suicides, desertions and family disorganization.

I heard numerous stories of how this law brought into light secret liaisons. Instances were common of seemingly submissive wives getting up in courts to declare: "I never loved my husband. I was forced into this marriage. Mr. X. has been my lover all these years. I want a divorce so that I can marry him now."

A law such as the New Marriage Law could easily have got out of hand and totally disorganized the community, uprooting as it did the accepted, traditional mores of the country. But it must be said to the credit of the People's Government that they watched the domestic revolt and the marital changes carefully to prevent anything like liberal morals becoming the order of the day. On the contrary, today the relations between the sexes, while no longer Confucian and traditional, have become almost prim and puritanical. Although premarital dating and courting are slowly spreading (and even social dances are being encouraged by the government), there is no laxity in morals as we understand it.

Already one sees in China the effects of this reform of enforced equality between men and women. Women work in literally every department of the nation's expanding economy. On the train that took me to Canton from Shum Chun, the frontier station north of Kowloon, I noticed that, for the most part, the guards, conductors, ticket collectors, cleaners, and, of course, the waitresses were women. The only one who is fairly certain to be a man on the railway staff is the engineer. When I reached Canton, the first person to jump into my compartment was a young lady Intourist guide who was to be my inseparable companion and interpreter for the next three days in Canton. Wherever I went, whether it was to visit textile and jute mills, machine tool factories and rubber factories, steel mills, farms, and mines, or government offices, I found women working alongside men and often outnumbering them. They worked on equal terms, both in positions of responsibility and in the heavy manual jobs that the non-Communist countries consider unfit for women.

Across the nation is scattered a network of nurseries and creches staffed with cooks, nurses, and teachers to care for the infants and children of women workers. Creches are attached to the various industrial establishments so that women can be free of their infants and able to work, and even nursing mothers have jobs, leaving their work for half an hour every four hours to nurse their babies.

It was the same story in clinics, nursing homes, and hospitals. While there were not many women doctors—they are now being trained—almost all the ancillary medical personnel were women.

I saw women guarding airports, bridges, and factories. There are women in the police—controlling traffic, watching the frontiers, detecting crime. There are women in diverse capacities in the People's Army, Navy, and Air Force.

As for manual labor, which Chinese women have done for centuries, it continues to be women's monopoly. Whether the government is laying roads or building bridges, putting up factories or raising dams, or just digging ditches, literally thousands of women work on these projects. One sees scores of women standing in a circle around a heavy stone, pulling the attached ropes in unison to make the stone bounce up and down to stamp the earth. A road-rolling engine could do this quicker and better, but China is yet to be mechanized. Woman-power is cheaper than machines. One sees almost everywhere—for China today is one vast building site—women carrying mud and a myriad other things slung on poles over their shoulders. This is, of course, tedious and inefficient, and the wheelbarrow is gradually coming into use to replace "pole power," but it is the women who push the wheelbarrows.

And last, and perhaps most important, women are active members of the Party. According to a recent estimate, there are nearly 1,000,000 women members in the Chinese Communist Party. And once women have been converted to Communism, there is nothing to stop the contagion of their conversion. It is these women who at Party meetings denounce their husbands' bourgeois deviations in thinking. It is these women who spy on their neighbors and report to the Street Committees.

Of course, like all revolutions, the Chinese Communist Revolution has produced a few women leaders. One might expect China's First Lady to be Madam Mao. But she, his fourth wife and a former Shanghai actress, is seldom seen in public for the simple reason that a woman does not become important in China simply because she is the wife of someone important. She must be distinguished in her own right. And the country's First Lady really seems to be the widow of Dr. Sun Yat-sen, second sister of Madam Chiang Kai-shek, and one of People's China's six Vice-Chairmen. She occupies a dignified position and, among the Soong sisters, was the only one to throw in her lot with the Communists. Her revolutionary husband is possibly the

one man that both the Kuomintang and the Communists
revere. No wonder that his widow should be something of
an elder stateswoman today.

Another important woman in China today, though not so
well known as Madam Sun Yat-sen, is Madam Chou En-lai,
otherwise known as Teng Ying-chao, Vice-Chairman of the
All-China Women's Democratic Federation. Others, more
known to the outside world as members of the cabinet, are
Madam Li Teh-chuan, the Minister for Health, and Madam
Shih Liang, the Minister for Justice.

III

Another reform effected by People's China, incredible in
its scope and seeming success, is the abolition of prostitution.
Soon after I arrived in Shanghai, I was asked whether I
would like to visit the Prostitutes' Reformation Institute. It
was pointed out that, as a social scientist, I ought to be
interested in this question, for Communist China had, they
said, really done away with the oldest profession. As I was
pressed for time in view of my other interests, I asked
whether it was possible for me to meet the Director of the
Institute at my hotel so that she could give me the details
of the reform and its *modus operandi*. My request was
granted, and the Director, a meek little woman in blue,
wearing glasses and carrying a pile of papers, called on me
at the hotel.

"Welcome to Shanghai," she said. "But how is it you
don't want to come to the Institute? Whatever I say may
sound second-hand. There is nothing like talking directly
to the women themselves, the prostitutes who are reformed
and who are eternally grateful to Chairman Mao and to
Communism."

"Did you ever visit Shanghai before Liberation?" she
wanted to know. I said I had, briefly, some years ago. "Then
you know what a horrible, whore-ridden city Shanghai

was." I replied that I did know something about it. "But I would like to know how you cleaned it up," I asked. "Did you take a census to begin with to know the size of the problem?"

She told me that no official census had been taken, for there was really no need, since everybody knew who was a public prostitute or a kept woman.

"When we moved into Shanghai, the cadres had already prepared a list of all public women. There were some 4,000 official prostitutes and some 30,000 'secret' or 'hidden' prostitutes. They were all rounded up into the Center, which for several weeks became something like a hospital. Few women were really healthy, and almost everyone was suffering from different stages of venereal disease. They were given the best treatment, and soon every woman was physically rehabilitated."

"Did these women have any homes left anywhere in China?" I asked. "Yes, a thousand or so had homes in the villages. Those who were willing to go back and whose relatives were willing to receive them were promptly sent back after a few weeks of educational reorientation."

"What kind of educational reorientation?" I asked.

"Mostly political education—some Marxist-Leninist principles of the new society," she said. Prostitutes lectured on the labor theory of value!

"And those who had no homes outside Shanghai were sent to the educational Center especially set up to re-educate these fallen women. They were taught various skills, based on their age, ability, and aptitude. They were taught anything from sewing and nursing to machine-operating and working in textile mills. They were quick to learn, and once they had mastered some skills, jobs were found for them, and off they went to lead respectable lives as workers. But most important was the ideological training imparted to these women. This new Communist education gave them self-respect, dignity, and love for Chairman Mao and the

People's Government. We thus mentally rehabilitated the whole lot."

"Did all the women readily fall into line, or did you have any disciplinary problems?" I wanted to know.

"A few at the beginning," she admitted. "Some ran away from the Institute but came back of their own accord for they could not make a living anywhere by their old ways. The prostitutes themselves formed a committee and no ex-prostitute could leave the Center until her departure was approved by the committee. When almost everyone had left the Center, there were still a few who did not want to leave the Center at all and to face the world. We did not know what to do at first, but we solved the problem by converting the Center into a factory. Now the women who did not want to go anywhere work happily in this factory."

"Have any of these women married and set up homes?" I asked.

"Many of the women are now married and have homes and children," she beamed. "We still continue to get letters from them thanking Mao's government for making new women out of 'ghosts.'

"Have you a serious prostitution problem in India?" she inquired. I said that we have the problem in most big cities, but the magnitude was negligible.

"Have you visited any big capitalist cities in Europe or America and studied the problem there?" she asked. "I believe such cities as New York, Paris, and London have not even begun to solve the problem of prostitution."

I said I had visited many European and American cities but had not particularly studied the problem. It was true, I admitted, that the capitalist cities had not solved it.

"One must have seen Shanghai before Liberation to believe it," she went on. "About five out of every hundred people were prostitutes, pimps, vagabonds, thieves, or pick-pockets. Life was not safe. People could not carry money about—pens and pocketbooks, watches and wallets disappeared. Believe it or not, in pre-Liberation Shanghai even people disappeared mysteriously. *Now* all this has been changed, as you can see for yourself. *Now* all the anti-social elements have been rehabilitated and given suitable jobs.

"Shall I tell you the life of a typical Shanghai prostitute before the Communist Liberation?" she volunteered.

"She was a young and pretty village girl of about fourteen years. She was the daughter of a landless farmhand. The landlord took her as his concubine but ill-treated her in various ways. Then a Shanghai woman, a typical pimp and madam, canvassing the countryside for new recruits, heard about the plight of the girl and managed to meet her. She pretended to help her and offered to obtain a good job for her in one Shanghai's textile mills. The woman helped the girl to escape to Shanghai. But, on arriving there, she was put into a prostitutes' home and asked to sign a piece of paper, with the assurance that it was the usual thing to do. The illiterate girl took it to be a contract and promptly signed it. Then she discovered that she had to sleep with all sorts of men. Prostitution was an organized big business. She protested, but she was beaten. Once she ran away to the British concession, but the police brought her back to the prostitutes' home. The police pointed out that they could not help her, since she had sold herself away according to the document she had signed.

"She had to receive as many as twenty men a day. Twice she became pregnant, but she had to undergo abortions which left her sick and limp. Even in such conditions she had to receive men. These women were not human beings but ghosts of their former selves. All these women have now been rehabilitated, thanks to Chairman Mao."

I commended her on this achievement, but asked her how they managed to deal with amateur prostitutes.

"We have our ways. Do not forget that the People's

Government receives 100 per cent support. We have our Street Committees and various organizations. The neighbors spy if a woman misbehaves. She is then denounced."

So that was it. Every woman spied on every other woman! And since everyone knows everyone else's business, how could anyone be a prostitute? No wonder that, in less than a decade, the world's oldest profession had been abolished, or rather almost abolished. For, in Canton, I learned that prostitution among the boat people on the Pearl river still continued to be something of a problem.

5
The New Education

Perhaps the most powerful weapon in the hands of a government to mold the people's thinking is educational organization. Nowhere has this fact been better understood, nor greater advantage taken of it than in the totalitarian countries of both the right and the left—as in Russia today or in Hitler's Germany, Tojo's Japan, and Perón's Argentina in the past. And during my travels in Communist China, I discovered that Mao was trying his hardest to mold the reading habits, thinking, and behavior of 700,000,000 people, from young children to old people, through a "New Education" that will fit them into the regimented pattern of socialist reconstruction.

A formal educational system normally includes all the organized and systematized instruction imparted to a person from the age at which he enters school till he formally graduates, or even after graduation if necessary. In the larger social sense, it begins when the child is born, and goes on throughout life. After one leaves school or college, the so-called formal education may end, but conscious and unconscious education through such organized mass media as the press and the platform, the film, radio, and television continues. China, like almost all countries, exercises control over formal education through the careful selection and preparation of courses and curricula, teachers and textbooks. But, in addition to this, and unlike in the democracies, all the mass media are rigorously controlled by the State, and education in the broader sense has become a State monopoly.

Wherever I visited a creche or a kindergarten—and these are numerous, attached to factories and farms, communes and mills—I was invariably greeted by the joyous clapping of tiny hands which was always a prelude to the enthusiastic singing of such familiar choruses as "Socialism Is Good" or "Communes Are Good" or "Chairman Mao Is Our Savior." Like all those bent upon thought control, the Chinese Communists believe in catching them young, and from the kindergarten on up to the university there is the inevitable strongly Communist-biased instruction. An educational system embraces everything that is imparted to students from the infant class onwards. While I tried to observe as much as I could of Chinese education at all levels, my interests were especially confined to what might be called higher education in the sense of colleges, universities, and research institutes.

II

In 1950, China had about 134,000 university students. Today, there are probably some 150,000 students in China's 185 universities and institutions of higher learning for a population of 700,000,000. That is, Communist China has one university student for every 5,000 persons.

I went around several medical, engineering, and what are called water conservancy colleges, as well as universities of different types in most of the cities I visited, and I discovered something decidedly abnormal about university education in China. All the liberal arts colleges and universities have abolished their liberal arts courses, or at any rate discontinued them. That is, the traditional courses offered in most universities of the world in such subjects as economics, politics, history, sociology, statistics, and anthropology are not being offered, and the members of these faculties and the students have been assigned various tasks on the nation's far-flung farms and in the factories. On inquiry, I learned that the production of food and other goods was more important than the turning out of graduates in these "useless" subjects. It is true that the immediate

needs of the country are food and manufactures and not
historians and sociologists, especially when history and sociology have not yet been recast to suit the needs of Chinese
Communist ideology.

Interestingly enough, the only liberal arts course being
taught in many universities is in linguistics and phonetics.
This is not as odd as it seems at first, for the Communists
are faced with the problem of language and communications: with a predominantly illiterate population speaking
numerous dialects, the question of communication between
the north and the south on the one hand and between the
majority and minority nationalities on the other has assumed
considerable national importance. The writ of the central
government in Peking in both the spoken and written language has to be understood in places as far removed as
Harbin and Lhasa, Lanchow and Shanghai.

The Peking dialect has been made the nation's official
language, and attemps to reform the script have been undertaken. In fact, a beginning has been made in introducing
the Roman script. I saw some secondary schools teaching
the English alphabet. And once the Roman script takes the
place of the Chinese pictographic and ideographic script, the
problem of a single national language and script will have
been solved. Hence the importance attached to the course
in linguistics and phonetics. It is a practical course and is
of compelling importance in cementing national unity.

But for the teachers and students belonging to this course,
the liberal arts colleges looked quite deserted. However,
I was assured that this was a temporary phenomenon and
that when the national emergency regarding production
was over, within a decade or so, liberal arts courses would
be restored in all the colleges.

In the place of the conventional liberal arts universities,
a new kind of college and university (these terms are often
interchangeable in China) has emerged. These are called
Red and Expert Schools. They are also sometimes known

as "People's Universities." The twin objectives of these schools, as the title "Red and Expert" indicates, are to mold the students enrolled in these institutions into sound Communists and experts in various skills.

No minimum formal education is needed to enter these institutions. One need not have passed the secondary-school examination or, for that matter, have attended any school at all. I met at these centers young as well as old farmers and industrial workers drawn primarily from the rural areas. These people would have been denied any kind of formal education in old China, and for them things have definitely changed for the better.

The instructions imparted to these students, who feel by and large somewhat self-conscious and awkward within the portals of a school, are at two unrelated levels. They are taught Communism—its genesis, growth, and development—and are also given a course or two on Marxist economics and politics and the history and problems of Communism.

At the second level, they are taught all that is necessary and possible in their particular fields of specialization—mostly semi-skilled jobs. It may be plowing or pottery, tinkering or welding, but whatever the job, the aim is to make the persons extremely proficient in it. The lessons are designed to make the student an expert, and though he does become an expert in his particular field, he knows nothing else. In short, he becomes a fanatical Communist and an expert mechanic. He becomes a Red and an Expert!

The third type of institution, which conforms more or less to those in the free countries, is represented by what are called technological universities. These embrace anything from a polytechnic and an engineering college to a steel institute and a national physics laboratory. Before the Liberation, these were few and far between. But during the last ten years, they have mushroomed all over the country thanks to the "selfless help" of the Soviet Union and, on a lesser scale, of East Germany, Czechoslovakia,

Poland, and other Iron Curtain countries. For instance, the former American-supported Tsinghua University has become a modern and well-equipped technological university. Some of the former traditional colleges in Harbin, Wuhan, Chengchow, Peking, Shanghai, and other cities have been converted into large engineering and technological universities. In addition to these, specialized technical schools for training in steel, textiles, precision instruments, and water conservancy have been opened at places where such skills are greatly needed.

These colleges, which offer courses from physics at the intermediate level to mathematics at the Doctor of Science level, have both Chinese and foreign professors, the aliens being either Russians or East Germans. The equipment in the laboratories appeared to be adequate. The students seemed to work very hard and led Spartan lives. But they are the privileged ones—the new class of Marxist technocrats who will industrialize and modernize China.

III

Throughout China's turbulent history of the rise and fall of empires and dynasties, Peking, whether it was the nation's capital or not, has been the country's cultural and educational capital. In modern times, Peking came to boast of four universities, and of these only the Peking National University, or Peita (Peita, pronounced something like "Baydah," is the abbreviation of Kuo-li Pei-ching Ta-hsueh, which means National Peking University), was in every sense thoroughly Chinese. It was proud and nationalistic and tried to impart all that was best in China's cultural heritage. It was, in fact, a center of leftist intellectual activity. Peita was within the walls of the old city of Peking, where poor students received the best classical education available in China from some of her greatest scholars. The university had presidents of the caliber of men like Dr. Chiang Monlin, now Chairman of the Joint Commission on Rural Reconstruction on Taiwan, and Dr. Hu Shih, who later was Kuomintang Ambassador to the United States and who is now, alas, a sad intellectual refugee from the People's Republic.

Then there was Yenching University in the countryside near Peking, supported by American funds and with close ties with Harvard. This was "Harvard-in-China" but not China's Harvard. Its lovely campus with bridges and lakes, gardens and villas, was, I learned, at one time the neglected but beautiful residence of a Manchu prince, and it was a stroke of genius for the Americans to get possession of it for their Yenching University. Dr. Leighton Stuart, that dedicated American student of China, was for many years its President, and a number of present-day Communist leaders passed through his hands from the portals of this university. There were many Americans and Europeans on its faculty, and it catered to the sons of well-to-do Kuomintang officials and wealthy businessmen; and also to a few foreign—primarily Western—students. I am not sure whether or not the students obtained a rigorous education, but they did learn something of Western manners and morals.

The third big university was Tsinghua, also more or less an American institution supported by Boxer Indemnity Funds. The fourth was Fu Jen, a Catholic institution run by European priests.

After the Liberation in 1949, American support for Yenching and other foreign institutions became impossible, and in 1952 Yenching was closed in the sense that the Peking National University moved out of its old and poor building into the well-appointed campus of Yenching. The area where Yenching formerly stood was really a suburb of Peking, and former residents recall that the surroundings of old Yenching were covered by little more than a few temples and innumerable graves. But today this area has radically changed. In the place of the scattered temples and graves now stand numerous new institutions. These, along with the Peking National University, have become what the Communists call Peking's Cultural Center, more or less an expanded version of the *cité universitaire* of Paris.

Unfortunately, on the evening that had been set apart for me to visit the Peking National University in the company of the Dean and three Indian students (who were learning the Chinese language there), I was told on arrival that we would be unable to go around as planned, for a Bulgarian Communist leader had passed away and the entire University was mourning his death. As I entered the main hall, I saw hundreds of students paying their respects to a huge portrait of the departed Bulgarian. I asked a student at random whom he was mourning. He replied, "I don't know his name, but he was a great People's Leader." This commandeered mourning prevented my programed visit's being carried through.

IV

"How does one obtain admission to these technological universities?" I asked the Dean of Tsinghua University in Peking, himself an engineer of some distinction. "We have given much thought to this question of admission," said the Dean, "and we have found that we could admit only the very best of our young men and women to become engineers and technologists." "Have you laid down any criteria for admission?" I asked. "Yes, we have three important criteria, and we follow them strictly. The first is that the prospective student must be oriented in socialist thinking; that is, he must be familiar with the Marxist approach to all our problems. Secondly, he must be in excellent health. The courses are strenuous, and we don't want students dropping out of the college for health reasons. And third and last, a student must have the requisite intellectual ability to cope with his studies."

"I can understand the second and third criteria, but how do you judge a candidate regarding the first?" I asked. "We have our ways. We keep tabs on the students right from their high school days. We know who is enthusiastic about socialism and the present regime and who has merely accepted the present order as inevitable. The convinced and enthusiastic are likely to become active and prominent members of the Communist Youth League. We know who is a real Communist and who is not among the students."

That was it. It was not enough if the student had the necessary aptitude, ability, and inclination to become a good physicist or geologist. He had to be a good Marxist physicist or an ardent Communist geologist.

Once the students are admitted to the portals of the technological institutions, their organized indoctrination begins. One would think that this was unnecessary, since only the converted among the youth are admitted. But the authorities are taking no chances. The student is exposed to the labor theory of value and the materialistic conception of history with the same vigor as he is to higher algebra and thermodynamics.

All the normal needs of the students are taken care of, though there is nothing luxurious about the accommodation, clothing, or food provided in the hostels; on the contrary, these appeared to be Spartan and uniform and without any diversity or variety.

In Canton, I visited the well-known southern university, Chungshan (one of the given names of Dr. Sun Yat-sen). The Assistant Dean told me that, since Liberation, the university had grown enormously in buildings, equipment, and, of course, in student enrollment and faculty strength. What the Dean did not tell me was that Chungshan University had taken over (like Peita in Peking) the buildings, the library, and the entire equipment of the old Ling Nam University, a well-endowed American institution. Ling Nam is no more, and its assets have been transferred to Chungshan

University without even a word of thanks to the Americans
who had built it up through the years.

V

A singularly unacademic feature of the colleges and universities that forcibly strikes a foreign observer is that the
heads of all of them are invariably fervent and seasoned
Party men. Normally one expects the head of an academic
institution to be either a distinguished scholar or an eminent
educator or at least an able administrator. But one discovers
in Communist China that the heads of even technical schools
and colleges are not necessarily scientists or engineers—they
are always veteran revolutionaries or prominent non-aca-
demic Communists.

Wuhan University is a typical example of this. In People's
China, the city of Wuhan has become famous for four attrac-
tions. The first is the huge iron and steel plant. The second
sight is the impressive Soviet-constructed bridge over the
great Yangtze river. The third important attraction is the
Heavy Machine Tool Plant, and the fourth is the university.

The university was not a post-Liberation affair but was
founded in 1913 as the Wuchang Sun Yat-sen University.
The campus enjoys a picturesque location. The beautiful
buildings, typically Chinese in architecture, rise on the undu-
lating Lo-ka hills beside the rippling and shimmering East
Lake. An ideal environment for study, work, and living.

The President of the University, a stocky man in his fifties
in the inevitable blue uniform, looked more like a retired
prize-fighter than a professor or college president. Over
innumerable cups of green tea and homemade cigarettes
in his well-appointed office room, he made me an impas-
sioned little speech:

"Before Liberation, there were less than a thousand students in this university. In 1952, as part of the reorganization
of the educational institutions throughout the country, the

university expanded to some twelve departments and three independent colleges of engineering, agriculture, and medicine.

"There are now 3,700 students, of whom 45.4 per cent come from worker or peasant families. Women students constitute 15 per cent. The faculty consists of 450 members.

"Since the rectification campaign and especially since the Second Plenary Session of the Eighth Party Congress proposed the general line of socialist construction, great results have been achieved in carrying out the educational policy—namely, education must serve politics, and education must be combined with productive labor. Much valuable experience has been gained in carrying out this educational reform of integrating politics with studies, combining theory with practice, education with production, mental work with manual work.

"Up to the present, this institution has set up over a hundred small factories and farms to provide students with opportunity for participation in labor. These enterprises include iron works, a building materials plant, a chemical plant, and farms producing a variety of products. Because of the utmost exertions of students and teachers, the emancipation of their minds, and the throwing overboard of their superstitions, some of their scientific researches as well as their experimental products have reached and even surpassed advanced world levels.

"At present, in this university, struggle on the educational front is being carried on, the struggle between the two roads, the two lines, and the two different points of view of the capitalist and the socialist. Educational reform is proceeding in a deeper and a more thorough way. We are thus endeavoring to build a new Communist Wuhan University."

After this speech, he poured me some more tea and asked me if I had any questions to ask or any "friendly criticism" to offer. I wanted to know where he had been trained and what his field of specialization was.

"I am the new President of this university," he told me. "I have had no academic training, for I have been all my life a revolutionary Communist soldier."

VI

A new slogan has recently been introduced into the Chinese educational system; I saw on every campus banners and posters proclaiming: "Education Must Be Combined with Productive Labor." This departure was one of the two measures introduced into China's school system at the end of last year. The principle was novel enough, for the Director or Assistant Director of every educational institution that I visited, from Sun Yat-sen University in Canton to Heilungkiang University in Harbin, harped on this theme.

The other measure introduced last year and which was in the process of implementation during my visit was the establishment of Agricultural Middle Schools. I visited a couple of these institutions. They are modeled after trade schools or technical or vocational high schools, and young working farmers of both sexes receive some practical training in the three R's of Chinese agricultural methods on a part-work and part-study basis. The practice of working while studying aims at combining ordinary schooling with productive labor. It breaks the age-old scholastic Chinese, or for that matter Asian, tradition of looking down on manual labor.

This new movement has led to the dissolution of schools and colleges as one ordinarily understands them. It is not that students do some part-time work of their own choice to earn a bit of money. This should not therefore be confused with what the Americans call "working one's way through college." Nor is it to be equated with Mahatma Gandhi's well-known Wardha scheme of a craft-biased education.

This "study with productive labor" is based purely on the Marxist theory of education, a welcome theory for present-day China, which does not have the resources in buildings, books, and teachers to educate her entire population of school-going age.

Karl Marx, in the first volume of his *Das Kapital*, talks about "an education that will, in the case of every child over a given age, combine productive labor with instruction and gymnastics, not only as one of the methods of adding to the efficiency of production but as the only method of producing fully developed human beings." Writing on another subject, *The Directives to the Delegates of the Provisional Central Council on Some Questions*, Marx observes: "In a reasonable social order, every child must become a productive worker starting at the age of nine." He goes on to suggest that "children from the age of nine to twelve should do two hours' work every day in a workshop or at home, children from thirteen to fifteen years of age four hours, and from sixteen to seventeen years of age six hours." He believed that "the combination of remunerative productive labor, mental education, physical exercise, and polytechnical training elevates the working class considerably above the level of the higher and middle classes." Marx pleads for this repeatedly in his writings. In his *Critique of the Gotha Program*, he observes: "An early combination of productive labor is one of the most potent means for the transformation of present-day society."

Lenin faithfully echoes this Marxist belief in ideal education. He says: "It is impossible to visualize the ideal of future society without combining the training and education of the young generation with productive labor. Neither training and education without productive labor, nor productive labor without parallel training and education could have been raised to the height demanded by present-day techniques and the state of scientific knowledge."

All this Marxist-Leninist thought on education is sum-

marized by Chairman Mao when he says that the aim of
Communist education in China is to produce "a cultured,
socialist-minded worker." A Chinese official explained to me
the meaning of Mao's term thus: "A cultured, socialist-
minded worker is a man who is both politically conscious
and educated. He is able to undertake both mental and
manual work. He is what we regard as developed in an
all-around way, both politically and professionally qualified.
He is a worker-intellectual and an intellectual-worker." In
other words, any educational policy which divorces mental
labor from manual labor cannot meet the demands of a
Communist society.

The Chinese interpretation of Engels' theory that labor
creates the world is something like this: "Physical labor
happened before mental labor. The latter is therefore based
upon the former and is of secondary importance. We must
completely weed out the bourgeois theory of the superiority
of mental to physical labor and must realize that physical
labor is the most important thing under the sun."

The fidelity and vigor with which the Chinese leaders are
translating this Marxist view into action reveal that the
faithful believe in the complete relevance of Marxist doctrine on education to present-day China's needs. It is no
wonder that China is waging a war against the intellectuals
and against anyone who maintains that "education should
be led by the experts" or that "professors and educators
must head and run the schools."

When this Marxist view of education is grasped, one easily
understands why the heads of even technological colleges
and universities are seasoned Party men or revolutionary
Communist soldiers. I met many professors who seemed to
apologize for their past academic training, which was "mere
acquisition of textbook knowledge" divorced from the reali-
ties of the people's needs. These professors are now making
amends by working on farms and in factories in the mornings
or evenings or during the weekends. They included teachers

from almost all disciplines. The new outlook is work—not the armchair or ivory-tower variety—but work that produces something tangible or directly serves the workers.

VII

In Shanghai, I wanted to visit the old and formerly American-supported St. John's University. I had gone around this university once years earlier and had met some of its graduates in American universities. I was told that this university had been transformed into the new Shanghai Academy of Social Sciences. I expressed a desire to visit it since this was the only institution (apart from the Institute of Economic Research in Peking, which I had the pleasure of addressing) devoted to study and research in social sciences—subjects which receive such low priority in the new China.

We drove to the academy, and I was received by two Vice-Directors, former professors at the university who continued to teach in addition to their administrative duties. The first Vice-Director, Dr. Lin, is an economist, a graduate of London University, and was at the London School of Economics between 1935 and 1937. The second gentleman, Dr. Pan, received his doctorate in political science from the University of Vienna in 1935. They both apologized for having forgotten English and German respectively, and our conversation was carried on through my inseparable companion and official interpreter who was assigned to me the day I arrived in Peking and who traveled with me all over China.

As we went around the various buildings, I noticed that these were more or less deserted.

"Is today a working day?" I asked.

"Yes, indeed, today is a normal working day."

"How many students are enrolled here?" I queried.

"About 4,600 in all."

"Are they all on this campus?"

"Technically yes, because they are enrolled here, but about 2,000 are working in the factories in Shanghai."

"Is it part-time work?"

"No. They put in eight hours in the factories. But they take a course once a week."

"What about the other 2,600 students?" I wanted to know.

"Another 2,000 are working on the farms on the outskirts of Shanghai."

"Do they come for the weekly course?"

"No. They will come back to the campus in a year or two when the temporary food problem has been solved."

"This means you have some 600 regular students actually here?"

"Not quite," replied the Vice-Director, "because some 200 are on steel duty. That is, the campus has set up a cottage-style steel furnace, and they are making steel."

Later we visited this traditional-style steel plant. It was just a furnace that was melting all the scrap metal gathered in by the students.

"The rest are regular students, I suppose."

"No, another 200 are practicing in the Student Militia, for they are assigned to join the Fukien Front." Here the Vice-Director gave me a little lecture on American imperialism and the necessary chore of shelling Quemoy and Matsu in the imperative task of "regaining" Taiwan.

Finally we entered a building where some student activity was discernible.

"This is the economics lecture hall," volunteered the Vice-Director. There was no lecturer present, but some twenty students were poring over books. The Vice-Director told me that he taught the course on "History of Economic Thought." I informed him that I myself had taught the same course for some years, and we began discussing the scope of the course, the textbooks adopted, and the favorite writers and questions of the students. "In India, we begin with Adam Smith and end with Keynes, though, of course, a few lectures are devoted to such economic thought as there was among such early Hindu writers as Manu and Kautilya."

"That is the conventional course we have been taught in the West," he conceded. "But we have changed all that since Liberation. Our 'History of Economic Thought' begins with Marx and ends with Chairman Mao."

"What writers do you specifically study?" I inquired.

"Marx, Engels, Lenin, Stalin, and Chairman Mao," was the reply.

We visited the economics seminar room, where a discussion was in progress among a score of students. There was no professor present, but the student leader invited us to join them, and we did. I was told that these were advanced students.

"Do they write an examination or submit a thesis?" I asked.

"They do both; but these students are working on a thesis," I was told.

At random, I asked a student what the subject of his thesis was.

"We don't have different subjects, for all of us are working on a single thesis," was his answer.

The Vice-Director intervened and informed me that the whole class works on a single thesis—a kind of cooperative effort.

"What is the subject of this collective thesis?"

"The communes," was the reply.

"Is there any objective evaluation of this collective thesis?" I asked.

"Oh, yes. The whole class criticizes the thesis and points out the deviations."

"But you said the whole class writes the thesis."

"That's right."

There was nothing else to do but change the subject.

Though I was told at every campus that the students had

regular terminal and annual examinations, I could never
find a question paper. Some professor or other was always
trying to find me a question paper, in the Chinese language,
or course, but they never seemed to manage it. At the University of Wuhan, the President had informed me that the
question papers were kept at the Ministry of Education in
Peking! Even last year's question papers!

After much discussion at various campuses, I discovered
that question papers and examinations have been abolished
for the present. No degrees or diplomas were granted. After
a prescribed course of study, the student was sent to some
school or office, factory or farm to do the work for which
he had been trained. If he didn't learn his job properly and
fumbled at his new occupation, it was just too bad. And yet
no professor would concede that this was the true state of
affairs in present-day China.

VIII

The head of the Shanghai Medical School told me that
they were turning out a new kind of medical graduates—
men who fulfilled the revolutionary aims of Communism in
the medical field. I asked what they were. "In pre-Liberation
China," he answered, "doctors attended the privileged few
who could afford to pay the doctors' fees. But the doctor
today serves the workers and the producers. This is possible only under Communism." I asked him whether he knew
anything about the comprehensive and free health services
in Great Britain. He was not aware of them.

"Another innovation," he pointed out, "is for the doctors
not to wait for the patients, but to go in search of them, as
in the communes. It saves the time of the worker." "What
about the doctor's time?" I asked. "That is, when the doctor
is free. When he is free, there is no point in his sitting around
waiting for the patients to come."

"It is the same in research work, too," he assured me. "In

pre-Liberation China, the few good research workers were spending all their ability, energy, and time in finding out about the rich people's diseases and nothing about the workers' diseases. Medical research had a class bias. Now we have changed all that."

Another aspect of general education in China is the strict control exercised over the production of books, pamphlets, and periodicals and printed matter in general. It is true that the total number of these has enormously increased during the last ten years. Newspapers catering to the needs and tastes of children, students, adults, farmers, industrial workers, office workers, Party members, artists, technicians, and so on are produced by the government. These give the "correct" news and views on all subjects relevant to the particular groups. It is the same with periodicals and magazines. I found the same official magazines—from comic books to journals devoted to the popularization of the sciences—in trains and planes, in homes and offices, in factories and on farms. One is greeted with the same official magazines no matter where one goes. When printing and publication become a State monopoly, no matter how it is defined, food for the mind becomes not only controlled but contaminated.

In colleges and universities the old books, mostly from the Western countries, have been thrown out, and one can see them dumped in some corner. The shelves thus emptied receive the authorized and approved books from the official sources in Chinese and books from Communist countries in such foreign languages as Russian and German. Even here, it is the Russian books that predominate over everything else. And among the countless books written on contemporary China in many languages, only a very few written by foreign Communists and approved by the People's Government are available. Now that the English language is officially disapproved, and since it will be many years before the Russian language can take its place, the Chinese are groping in what can only be called a "darkness at noon."

IX

The introduction of "thought struggle" and the reformation through it of all teachers at all levels was perhaps the
saddest and most humiliating part of the entire reorganization of China's educational system toward the creation of
the new Communist society. A series of public meetings was
held at all campuses, where professor after professor who
was not already an avowed Communist had to go on the
platform before students, fellow teachers, the Party cadres,
and the public and recant, in the most abject and debasing
terms, everything he had said, taught, or written all his life.
Many volumes could be compiled of these recantations, and
they would be fertile source material for the study of human
nature under duress for some competent social psychologist.
(The Communists themselves have published some four
volumes of collections of confessions: *Thought Reform Documents,* Peking: 1952). A few random examples will suffice
here.

Chen Yuan, a well-known senior Chinese Catholic his-
torian and president of the now-defunct Fu Jen (Catholic)
University in Peking, in an open letter to Dr. Hu Shih in
the *Progressive Daily* writes:

> [On reading Chairman Mao's works,] a new world has
> opened before me. I realize for the first time that our
> whole study of history has been subjective and unscien-
> tific. Man's mind is determined by his society. He must
> study that society in order to understand the individual
> and can reform the individual only through reforming
> the society. All culture follows politics and at the same
> time leads politics. The realization of this fact is the
> freedom that the [Communist] government has brought
> to me.

Professor Fung Yu-lan, a Chinese philosopher whose reputation was something like that of Dr. S. Radhakrishnan in

India, recanted all that he wrote in his books and denounced himself:

> Now I feel I also have been liberated. Marxism-Lenin-ism and the thought of Mao Tse-tung, as well as prac-tices in the various aspects of the new society, have changed my thought, turning me from reaction to rev-olution, from service to individuals to service to the masses, from abstract things to concrete things, from illusions to realities.
>
> Formerly I felt it strange that in the revolutionary camp a political leader should also be a philosophical and ideological leader, and attributed it to the results of controlled thought. Now I came to understand that a leader capable of leading revolution and leading society too in its forward progress is always able correctly to understand the laws of the world and social develop-ment and able to apply it [*sic*] flexibly to concrete revolutionary practice. That he is able to do so is pre-cisely because he establishes and develops, in the rev-olutionary practice of reforming the world, a revolu-tionary philosophy for reforming the world. A revolu-tionary philosophy for reforming the world is entirely different from the philosophy which maintains that it "interprets the world." It is precisely because of its in-ability to reform the world that it is also unable to in-terpret the world. I now came to understand that I should make an entirely new start in my study before I can make myself a philosophical worker in the new society. Formerly, when I heard some people saying that they wanted to be the pupils of Chairman Mao, it seemed an exaggeration to me. *But now I feel that I am even disqualified to be a pupil of Chairman Mao, and that I have to strive hard to be one.* [Italics mine.]

All the intellectuals and others in the academic world, from the university president and professor down to the

primary school mistress have turned themselves inside out,
confessing their past bourgeois sins of training, teaching,
and thinking, and proclaiming their new and zealous conversion to Marxism-cum-Maoism. Hail "the greatest and most
peerless" educationist of all times, Chairman Mao!

One evening at an Indian Embassy party in Peking, I was
introduced to a young European woman who was working
in her country's embassy in Peking. In the course of our
talk, I discovered that she had been a careful student of all
the self-abasement recantations in China during the last
nine years. I expressed my interest in the documents and
confessed that I had not read many of these recantations—
all of which have not been translated. She loaned me a bulky
manuscript which I perused with some care. It took me some
time to wade through the hundreds of pages of sickening
new sentiments of the scholars who now belied all their
scientific training and were groveling in the dust before
Mao. From these endless pages, two things stand out in my
mind. The first is that the mental third degree administered
by Communism can often reduce human beings to dithering
idiots and, secondly, that Mao is an incredible mixture of
Buddha and Christ, Newton and Einstein, Plato and Kant,
Hegel and Bertrand Russell, Garibaldi and Gandhi, Napoleon
and Nelson, and, of course, Lenin and Stalin—take your pick.
Mao is greater than all and any combination of them!

I believe there is a mental Gresham's Law. All the un-
desirable control and regimentation of thought drive out ennobling ideas of individuality and freedom.

I believe that the cultural standards and the intellectual
outlook of a country can be judged by the treatment meted
out to authors and books. And here Communist China has
failed miserably, for she has successfully choked the channels of intellectual communications between herself and the
world beyond the bamboo and iron curtains. The prevention
of the publication of books privately (even granting that
some Chinese author can still write anything smacking of

individual liberty and freedom) and the banning of all foreign books except those written by approved fellow travelers impose on the minds of China's millions a new slavery.

Perhaps the most distressing and devastating aspect of Communist education is that, while it instructs, it also forges fetters on men's minds with a calculated deliberation. While it is true that one can become an able physicist or a competent geologist under Communism, no one can obtain that broad, liberal, and humanistic education that only a free society can afford to impart to its citizens.

It is true that, through the ages, theocratic rulers and imperialistic regimes have tried to confine people to conventional modes of thinking. They have tortured, imprisoned, and killed those who rebelled against the accepted doctrines of the church or the State. In China's own history, we have the example of Shih Huang-ti, the usurper, who, wishing to pose before posterity as the first emperor, burned all the classical books and killed all the intellectuals. In the twentieth century, the British government has imprisoned at some time or other men like Gandhi, Nehru, and Bertrand Russell —men who had the vision to protest against existing forms of government and current notions of fashionable and respectable thinking. And yet, while these men were physically imprisoned, their minds were free. They could get the books they wanted and, what is more, some of the finest and loftiest prose of our times came from the pens of these prisoners. But under Communism not only the bodies of dissenting persons are imprisoned (or liquidated), but what is truly terrifying is that their minds, too, are imprisoned, drugged, and debased into a pathetic, colorless conformity.

6

The Changing Family

The years of shock treatment administered by the Chinese Communists have rendered virtually impossible any reconstitution of the pre-Liberation form of Chinese society. Of all the institutions that have been affected, the most important is the family.

What the cell is to the biological or organic body, the family is to society. The family in China, as in other parts of the world, has been the single major factor in ensuring the stability and survival of the essentials of human civilization. From the time of Confucius, China's emperors and philosophers realized its importance as a fundamental social unit and its tremendous role in determining the character and structure of society.

In the *Book of Poetry*, edited by Confucius, it is said: "No one is to be looked up to like a father. No one is to be depended on like a mother." During those Confucian times, certain "criminals" were held to be worse than murderers. They were: "the son who does not serve his father respectfully, but greatly wounds his father's heart; and the father who cannot cherish his son but hates him; and the younger brother who does not bear in mind the evident intention of Heaven, and will not respect his elder brother; and the elder brother who forgets the tender regard in which he should hold his younger brother, and is unfriendly to him."

Through the centuries these theoretical directives of good behavior and family loyalty gradually took root to the extent that not only business but even government became family matters. Men did not usually associate with strangers in any venture, but only with their kin. Until recently, almost every person employed in the great banks or textile mills of China, from the manager down to the errand boy, was a relative of the proprietor and from his own village. Family loyalty was so deeply ingrained that what is generally called nepotism had become a desirable and accepted social virtue. In China, the greatest loyalty was always given not to the State, or to religion, but to the smallest group—the family.

One aspect of the Communist assault on traditional Chinese society has been the technique of denunciation, destroying loyalty among relatives.

The campaign of denunciations began within two years of the Communists' seizure of power. On February 21, 1951, the government promulgated the "Regulation of the People's Republic of China for Punishment of Counter-Revolutionaries." This regulation was intended to suppress all opposition to the Communist regime and its policies, no matter what shape such opposition took or from what quarter it came. One extraordinary feature was that penalties were decreed for offenses committed before the promulgation of the measure.

A major effect of this regulation has been the demoralization of age-old familial loyalties. In the name of waging a war against anti-government counter-revolutionaries, the government in effect tried to break the bonds between husband and wife, parents and children, one relative and another. For the first time in China's long and checkered history it became a virtue and an imperative patriotic duty to bear witness against one's kith and kin.

Why did the Chinese give up their traditional and intimate loyalties so easily? The answer is simply that people do not like to face death. One can face social ostracism, economic disinheritance, and political persecution, but strong must be the soul that is ready to die for love of one's relations, especially when such love and emotion have been declared reactionary, unpatriotic, and unacceptable by society at large. The much-publicized open mass trials and

accusations became so terrorizing that the thought upper-
most in the mind of every Chinese once the drive had begun
was survival.

What was worse, if the regime took it into its head to
accuse any man of being a counter-revolutionary in thought
or deed, his wife was presumed guilty of collusion for not
publicly denouncing her husband, whether she knew the
husband to be guilty or not.

Chinese newspapers, magazines, films, and official pro-
nouncements of recent years record countless instances of
sons and daughters accusing their parents (interestingly
enough, few parents turned against their children) and
wives turning against their husbands, and sometimes vice
versa, all in the name of the patriotic duty of ferreting out
anti-government elements. Although such denunciations are
not now so widespread as during the height of the drive,
they still continue.

This drive has sown seeds of suspicion between one member and another in almost every family. Distrust has now
become the watchword, and one cannot confide one's
thoughts, not to speak of one's deeds, to another, however
intimate the relationship between the two may be. Mis-
carriage of justice, even as the Communists understand the
term, became enormous because old scores in villages were
frequently settled during this period by denouncing the
hated person as a counter-revolutionary.

The resulting "my-relative-might-be-a-spy" attitude was
naturally more discernible in the villages than in the cities.
I found the families I visited in rural homes extremely
reticent, and they spoke guardedly. One usually speaks up
only in a large company, thus ensuring that others hear one's
safe and noncommittal remarks. This reticence might also
have arisen from the fact that our conversation was always
carried on with the aid of an official interpreter and in the
presence of some head or official connected with the unit
to which the family in question belonged.

Imagine how far China has traveled under the Communists when we witness today the sons of the accused demonstrating their loyalty to the State not only by denouncing their father but by screaming with the crowd for his death. This incredible change in the thinking and behavior of the Chinese cannot be dismissed as a passing emotional aberration. It has been brought about by an intense nation-wide campaign of indoctrination—a campaign that has apparently succeeded in almost completely transforming the accepted codes of behavior in Chinese society. Thus demoralization has set in, disrupting the cherished values inherent in the traditional close family of the Chinese.

Another aspect of the assault on traditional society has been the emancipation of women, for, although this has included many desirable reforms, it has also contributed to the disruption of the old family system.

Arranged marriages have been abolished. Pre-marital meeting and courting are encouraged. A young man or woman can marry anyone of his or her choice provided the local Communist Party and precinct police raise no objections. Concubinage and prostitution have been strictly outlawed. Monogamy has become the rule. Women have also obtained freedom of divorce.

On the economic front, women can hold property—at least such property as is still permitted to private ownership. But perhaps the most important reform is that women's wages are paid directly to them, not to their husbands or fathers. I was told that this simple and just change in itself had reduced the family patriarch to an impotent position, and that male domination in the family had vanished.

The imposition of central authority has been an equally revolutionary change. The Chinese have been known throughout centuries for their rugged individualism. The people, particularly the rural folk, have gone about their daily business, through all their ups and downs, relying on their traditional knowledge and common sense, animated, if unconsciously, by the belief that they were governed best when they were governed least. They seldom came in contact with even provincial authority, not to speak of any directives from the nation's capital.

This age-old disregard for central authority is now gone entirely. Peking has tightened its hold on the remotest areas. In distant villages, people's contact with the thought, actions, and directives of the capital is alive, thanks to the radio. The nation's administration is now close-knit and Peking's directives are carried out speedily and efficiently all over the country.

The effects of all these changes can be seen most vividly in the commune, the most extreme form of communized society known. These communes have been set up in rural areas all over the country. Peking's official claim is that they include 90 per cent of the rural population—some 500,-000,000 people. My estimate is that, in fact, only 100,-000,000 to 200,000,000 are living communal lives. But government spokesmen frankly state that they will not rest until the whole country has become one vast commune. During my travels, I heard from many quarters that one of Chairman Mao's ambitious targets was to make the nation's capital—Peking—the first metropolitan commune in the world. According to some, his insistence on this was one of the reasons that led to his resignation as head of the State.

I had occasion to visit four communes—the northernmost was some sixty miles north of Peking and the southernmost was near Chengchow. Of the four, two were showplaces—one, the Sputnik Commune, and the other, Chi-li-ying, known as "The Commune of the Sixteen Guarantees." I spent a whole day in the latter and saw something of every aspect of the commune's life. Even Chinese delegations from different parts of the country have been visiting Chi-li-ying to learn how to organize a commune.

The Communists are not only not apologetic but positively

proud of the transformation wrought in Chi-li-ying over a short period of time. Here, they have not only challenged but have swept away the concepts of centuries. This "Commune of the Sixteen Guarantees" is the apotheosis of the collective and the ultimate in Communist organization of public ownership.

As we stepped out of the jeep, my interpreter, the city official from Chengchow who accompanied us, and I were cordially greeted by a stocky peasant in the inevitable blue uniform—the Director of the commune. He was very happy, he said, to welcome "the scientist from India, our great and friendly neighbor." As we walked to his modest rural office —the home of an ex-landlord—he observed that he himself was a good example of what Chairman Mao and Communism had done for the nation.

"Before the Liberation, I was the exploited son of a farmhand who never owned a *mou* of land. I did not know where India was. But now I am the People's Director and, thanks to intense study of world problems and international relations, I have come to know India as our great neighbor and friend who is fighting for China and peace."

We went around the commune—innumerable creches of chubby infants, kindergartens overflowing with well-fed children singing the now-familiar songs, "Socialism Is Good," "Communes Are Good" and "Chairman Mao Is Our Savior"; the Middle Schools and the Red and Expert Schools—all coeducational—and their attached hostels, clinics, and kitchens.

The Principal of the Red and Expert School was ebullient. "This kind of school is new and is not yet known even in other People's Republics," he told me. I asked him if there was nothing like this commune in Russia. "I don't think so," he replied. "Here we demonstrate that virtue is teachable and human nature can be changed. And learning here is no longer the privilege of the limited few but the birthright of all."

He asked me whether we in India had compulsory education for all. I pointed out that, while we have not yet
achieved anything like compulsory free primary or high
school education in India, the United States of America and
some European countries have more or less achieved these
goals.

We stopped at random at the home of a peasant. It was
a small mud affair, extremely clean and neat. We were introduced to a peasant couple in their thirties. They greeted
us by clapping their hands, and we reciprocated. They formerly had been what were called "middle" peasants, neither
rich nor poor. The house had three large rooms, which the
couple's sizable family had occupied before the commune
was organized. Now the family had been dispersed. The
couple, who previously owned the house, had been allotted
one room, and two other couples, strangers from a nearby
village, had moved into the two other rooms.

"My old parents have gone to the 'Happy Home for the
Aged.' My two sons are in the Middle School hostel. I am
happy for them because they are getting an education—the
new education that will make them experts. But it is the
baby I miss." The wife said this, looked at the official, and
added, "Of course, I can now work hard and happily, knowing that my baby is well taken care of."

"How old is the baby?" I asked.

"About three," was the reply.

"Can't you visit the baby?" I wanted to know.

"Of course, my husband and I can, and we do. But we are
so very busy with work, study, and meetings," she said, in
a tone half proud and half sad, "that we haven't very much
time for the baby."

"Of course, we realize that we have to work hard and
produce more to defeat the American enemy and get back
Taiwan," her husband intervened. His statement seemed
inspired by the presence of the official, but it is possible that
he meant it. In China, one gets so used to hearing statements

like this that I wasn't surprised to hear it from this young peasant.

"Everyone in this commune feels that way about our enemy and the Taiwan crisis. In fact, some of our workers are so patriotic that they refuse to rest after their work. We have to persuade them to go home and sleep. In capitalist countries, I am told, workers malinger, but our problem is the other way around," added the Director.

"Can you bring your child home if he falls ill?" I asked the mother.

"Of course, I can spend some time with my baby if he is ill, and if the person in charge of the creche sends for me," she replied.

In the creches we visited, the children did look happy and cheerful. Everything was clean and orderly, and the women in charge even wore cotton surgical masks. The children in their padded clothes—houses are very poorly heated all over China because of the fuel shortage—played with their crude commune-made toys.

I raised the question of children's illnesses and parental visits with the woman in charge of one creche. "We have a Western-trained, as well as a traditional, doctor," she said. "Both examine all sick babies and give them what is considered the best treatment under the circumstances. Sometimes we send for the parents, but more often not. We find their knowledge of how to care for their infants is certainly inferior. The doctor and nurse know more about what is good for the babies than do the parents."

"Don't you make allowances for the emotional needs of children for their parents and of parents for their children?" I asked.

"We have had no difficulties so far. There is no hard and fast rule, and the parents can certainly visit the children any time they want to. Don't forget that in the commune we are one big happy family."

Among the institutions we visited was a dormitory for

unmarried men and women. The occupants were roughly in
the twenty to twenty-five age group. Some were waiting to
get married and move into rooms allotted to married couples.

In this group was an occasional married man or woman.
The women were introduced as "Worker" or "Producer," not
as "Mrs. X." or "Mrs. Y." I inquired into the reason for separation. "The spouse is probably a very skilled worker and in
demand elsewhere in some other town," I was told. "But
the separation is temporary until the authorities can find a
suitable job for the partner in the same area." It is not un-
common to come across married women working on teams
in communities miles way from their husbands.

There is a belief outside China that the separation of husbands and wives sometimes found in the communes is a
deliberate one. Some external observers have jumped to the
conclusion that the communes are trying to solve the country's population problem (in other communes) through such
separations, but I inquired into this matter in some detail
and have satisfied myself that these separations are temporary and accidental and not designed by authorities for
any demographic purpose.

While discussing this aspect of life in the commune, the
Director pointed out: "We have a great many marriages in
this commune. Before the Liberation, economic insecurity
and parental disapproval were effective deterrents to a
young man's marriage even in rural areas. Usually the
parents arranged the marriage of the children to suit
parental convenience. All this has been changed. Now if the
young people fall in love, they can marry without any
trouble under the commune's auspices. And they can have
all the babies they want, subject only to the demands of
work, health, and study. All the children are the responsibility of the commune."

I visited a "Happy Home for the Aged" where one old
lady—about seventy, perhaps—offered me a handful of
shelled peanuts. "Are you happy here?" I asked.

"Oh, yes, I am; but I miss my grandchildren," she said, adding, perhaps as an after-thought, "I know they are getting a useful education somewhere."

Through their vague and indirect remarks—or more often through their silence at my questions—I could discern these people's unhappiness over the disruption of their families. In the past, there were times when they did not have enough to eat or enough blankets in winter, but this was more than compensated for by the warmth of family loyalty and affections. Those days are gone, and now they have material necessities but not emotional security.

Even the most casual observer could not have helped seeing that the average adult looked sullen and unhappy. He followed official directions and did his duty, but dejection and misery are impossible to conceal. We have incredible poverty in some of India's villages, but such poverty has never been a barrier to banter and humor, and even, oddly enough, gaiety. This I completely missed in the communes and the countryside of China.

The Director invited me to a simple but adequate lunch in his own office. It consisted of meat dumplings (*chia-tse*) which we dipped in a hot sauce, a sweet dish, and endless cups of hot tea. Everyone enjoyed the lunch, and the Director, obviously satisfied and happy, recalled his days as a landless farmhand in this village before the Liberation.

"These meat dumplings were a great luxury then, because we couldn't afford meat. We had this dish only once a year during a festive occasion. Now we can have this delicacy any time we want." And he served me a few more hot dumplings.

I asked the Director whether anyone could leave the commune for some other place in China. He was genuinely surprised at my question, as if the thought had never occurred to him.

"I cannot imagine anyone wanting to leave this place," he

replied. "Please don't forget that this commune came into existence because the people themselves demanded it."

He then explained that migration within China was controlled by a permit system. The permit goes with the ration card which enables one to buy rice, oil, and pork in the cities and other non-commune areas.

In the communes there is no need for ration cards because everybody eats in the common mess halls. Hence anyone leaving a commune—unless on official business or with special permission—would be unable to obtain food elsewhere. Furthermore, one of the duties of Street Committees is to inform their daily meetings of both new arrivals and persons missing from the community street. So desertion from the communes is hazardous. Anyone caught is usually condemned to hard labor in one of the remote areas which are being developed.

"Can one go out of the commune to visit friends or relatives?" I asked.

"Permission may be granted under special circumstances, but actually such requests have not come to me so far," the Director assured me.

In the commune, as almost everywhere in China, the people no longer talk freely among themselves, unless it is purely "official talk" about production techniques, the greatness of the new regime, or the need to defeat the "imperialist Americans." It is all the more rare for the Chinese to talk with a foreigner (even should they know a common language and find an opportunity to talk without the interpreter being present—an almost impossible situation), for one cannot be certain that the visiting foreigner is not a Communist and an admirer of the present regime. For aught they knew from the official reception given to me, I might have been the Secretary of the Indian Communist Party!

This is a model commune—"the latest development, where we have gone one step ahead of the Soviet Union," as officials in Peking repeatedly told me.

Everyone works according to his or her ability, and all are given their basic needs. Everyone's loyalty is dedicated to the all-powerful state and its demands and directives. Food, clothing, housing, education, medical care, recreation, and burial are guaranteed. What more can one ask for? The tentacles of the State embrace every aspect and account for every hour of one's life. Leisure, privacy, and solitude have become dreadful vices. Abiding emotional attachments are suppressed in the name of the new Moloch of State and production.

What is likely to be the end of this new way of life? Will the worm some day turn and a silent revolution of angry men and women overthrow the communes? Or will the communes evolve in time a new human species—robots that respond to the radio? It is rash to prophesy.

7
China's Population Problems

When the People's Republic of China announced on November 1, 1954, that it had conducted the first scientific census in the country's long history and that the nation had more than 600,000,000 people, the prosaic demographic fact became a sensational newspaper headline all over the world.

This news item had numerous repercussions. First, there were the skeptics who wondered whether the Communists had really conducted a census. Secondly, granting that a census had been successfully carried out, they wondered whether the government was giving the correct or a padded figure, for statistics under Communism have a certain strategic value. Thirdly, if the figure was even approximately correct, it followed that all previous academic and political analysis of China's economic and demographic picture was misleading, as it had been based on the assumption that her population was around 450,000,000.

Any analysis of China's population problem in the past was largely a hazardous, if not impossible, undertaking, for there was no authentic and reliable source material, such as a census series or continuous vital registration. No government in China in the past had undertaken this very necessary but difficult task of enumerating the population, nor of registering her births and deaths for the entire area.

The difficulties are obvious. A strong central government and political stability were absent. The edicts of the central government from the earliest dynasty to the KMT at Chungking and Nanking were not binding over the entirety of China. The area (even without the newly acquired Manchuria and Tibet and the so-called autonomous regions in the northwest) is vast; the terrain is difficult and at places inaccessible, and communications absent or primitive. Most of the people were illiterate and suspicious of anyone asking what might be construed as personal questions.

This does not mean that there had been no estimates of China's population in the past, but they are of no practical value in the sense we understand the concept "population estimate" today.

During the Han Dynasty (206 B.C.–220 A.D.), however, some detailed counts were made for purposes of taxation, military conscriptions, and slave labor. Later, in the time of the Sung Dynasty (960 A.D.–1279 A.D.), the *Pao Chia* system was introduced whereby every locality was divided into groups of households, with one man in each group made responsible for an annual return of the number of people under his control. The aim was to know the number of adult and able-bodied people for military and taxation purposes. The accuracy of these returns is, of course, questionable. But the system continued more or less down to the days of the Manchu Dynasty, and was, it is said, destroyed about a century ago when the Taiping Revolution broke out. The Manchu government, however, made an attempt at census before the Revolution of 1911 and published an estimate of 374,000,000 for the China of that day.

And in March, 1945, the Kuomintang government estimated the population to be 454,928,992. No one knows how it arrived at this figure, precise to the last digit. But we do know that there was no real census. It was on the basis of this misleading figure that China's population was taken to be 450,000,000 for all practical purposes. Despite this medium figure, one can compile an impressive list of estimates of China's population, ranging from 350,000,000 to the United Nations' figure of 500,000,000. These involved assumptions and calculations which could not be subjected to year, area, or the methods adopted in arriving at them.

It was, therefore, something of an achievement when the Communist government conducted a census in 1953-1954 for almost the whole of China and announced the high figure of 583,000,000 for the mainland. The total was given out as 602,000,000, but this includes estimates of 7,600,000 Chinese for Taiwan and 11,700,000 other Chinese outside the mainland.

A successful census of China is such a rare scientific event that the population figure became a sensation. The scientific world is, of course, grateful to the People's Government for carrying out the first systematic census. In Asia, the only two major countries with a long and distinguished record of official and decennial census series are India and Japan; China had been a question mark, but the answer was found at last. And it was a surprising answer, for obviously her population had been consistently and considerably underestimated during the last fifty years by all available statistical agencies.

Normally a nation's census holds no interest to anyone unless he is a demographer, statistician, or economist. But the Chinese census results have considerable interest not only to social scientists all over the world but to the governments and peoples in Southeast Asia, beyond the geographical confines of China.

I met in Peking some statisticians, economists, and administrators who were in charge of the census operations. Mr. Pai Chen Hua, an economist of the Chinese Academy of Sciences, told me: "No government in the past could have undertaken the census, for they could not get the support of the masses. It is true there was a kind of census once during the Manchu rule and once again during the Kuomintang regime, but they did not embrace the whole country and were not accurate. China's population was usually taken as 400,000,000. It was not an economic concept but a political one based on customs and post office estimates."

He continued: "After the Liberation, a preliminary survey

of China's population was undertaken, but the real scientific investigation was not undertaken on a nation-wide basis until 1953. The reason for choosing the year 1953 was that we had our general election during that year, and, in a sense, our real economic reconstruction began that year. In early 1953, unified measures were published by the State Council, and registration schedules were released. All information was gathered as of midnight June 30, 1953. And registration was on the basis of permanent residence.

"The census theoretically belongs to the Ministry of the Interior, but our first census was undertaken under the joint auspices of the Ministry of the Interior, the Ministry of Public Health, the State Statistical Bureau, and the Committee for General Election. (The State Statistical Bureau and the Commitee for General Election do not belong to any ministry. They come under the National People's Congress.)"

The census operation lasted for nearly eight months during 1953-1954, though the final count was given as of June 30, 1953. The total number of trained workers was 2,500,000. Besides these, thousands of "Activists" (members of the Communist Youth League) and members of various Party organizations helped the government locate the people and register them. Technical help was provided by Soviet experts who, in cooperation with the Chinese statisticians, drew up the simple census schedule and decided on the methods of registration.

Only those in very remote and inaccessible areas were not directly counted. The rural areas of the Sinkiang Uighur Autonomous Region, Tibet, Western Chinghai province, Western Szechuan province, and Western Yunnan province —all of which are relatively thinly populated—were surveyed indirectly on a sampling basis and, as the resulting number was only 8,000,000, the total figure for all of China was not seriously affected.

Numerous sampling checks at various stages of the census

were instituted. These revealed an omission of 2.5 per 1,000 persons and a duplication of 1.3 per 1,000. The sampling check covered a population of about 50,000,000.

The census schedule was a simple one. Unlike most countries including India, which ask twelve to sixteen basic questions, China restricted her questionnaire to four: name and relation to the head of the family, age, sex, and nationality.

The government considered the "nationality" of the citizen an important question. By nationality is not meant the citizen's national origin as much as what might be called ethnic or racial identity. In the past every Chinese passed for a Han (an overwhelming majority of the Chinese belong to this ethnic group) and did not disclose their true nationality because they were afraid of denials and discrimination, if not persecution. But since the People's Government not only does not discriminate but guarantees the cultural life of the various racial minorities, people returned their true ethnic origin in the census.

The census revealed that the Hans constituted 547,283,657 or nearly 94 per cent of the total Chinese population; of the remaining, 35,000,000 or about 6 per cent were claimed by the following ten nationalities: Mongolian, 1,400,000; Hui, 3,500,000; Tibetan, 2,700,000; Uighur, 3,600,000; Miao, 2,500,000; Yi, 3,200,000; Chuang, 6,600,000; Puyi, 1,200,-000; Korean, 1,100,000; Manchu, 2,400,000; and others, 6,700,000.

The census also revealed that males, as in most Asian countries, were in a majority, constituting 51.82 per cent.

As China has been an industrially underdeveloped country and a considerable part of her population is engaged in agriculture, the rural-urban composition as revealed in the 1953 census confirms the Asian pattern of occupational distribution. The urban population constituted 13.26 per cent and the rural population was 86.74 per cent.

The registration of the citizen's age presented some difficulties, for there is no commonly accepted uniform year in China. For the purposes of the census, it was decided that a person's age was to be calculated as that of June 30, 1953 (Gregorian calendar). But many in China use the Chinese calendar as well as local customs in counting their age. The Chinese do not generally calculate their age in completed years. They reckon the age of a newborn infant as one, and the infant becomes two at the New Year. Some people reckon the date of their birth in terms of the old twelve-year-cycle system (the year of the Tiger, the year of the Ox, etc.), and some are accustomed to count by the year of the dynasty in which they were born. But the census authorities solved this problem by the preparation of a special conversion table by which they could figure out the birth date of every person in a uniform way, from one year to a hundred years old.

The age data revealed that 36.7 per cent were fourteen and under, 47.2 per cent between fifteen and forty-nine, and 16.1 per cent were fifty and above. It is obvious that the Chinese population is a youthful one, with 36 per cent of the total being under fourteen years of age. A technical discussion of the implications of this fact in terms of the available labor force and the future growth of China's population cannot be entered into here, but anyone can see that, with the gradual decline of the death rate, this youthful population is bound to grow in numbers. New China will have at her disposal enough manpower for years to come.

The census was based on the "habitually resident" population, since the *de jure* population is more meaningful in the determination of the size of a community. However, allowance was made for the nation's traditional family system. In China, every member is regarded as an inseparable part of it, regardless of how far away he may be living or how long he has been away from home. "In order not to offend this feeling of family unity, it was decided to include in the count as 'permanent residents' all those

who at the time of the census had been living or were to
remain away from home for less than five months, in a
separate column which would not be used in making the
count. Actual registration of the long-absent members would
then be made in the places where they resided."

The first official census thus threw some limited but most
welcome light on China's demographic situation. In June,
1954, the Deputy Prime Minister announced the general
results and released a five-page document entitled *Report of
the Registration of the Nation-wide Census.* A few months
later the State Statistical Bureau published a twenty-eight-
page report called *Documents of the 1953 Census.* In contrast
to about a hundred volumes that the Indian government
publishes on its decennial census, these may appear juvenile,
but I believe that the Chinese government deserves to be
congratulated on this stupendous effort, for China in 1953
was less organized administratively than India in 1872 when
we first began our national census.

II

Although it is certainly true that China, prior to the present
regime, had no regular, nation-wide vital registration system, various efforts were made in the past to ascertain
China's birth and death rates for at least small areas. The
International Settlement in Shanghai attempted to collect
birth and death statistics as early as 1902, but it was not
totally successful. Some experiments on vital registration
were carried out by American academic and other bodies in
cooperation with Chinese universities and regional governments. The Scripps Foundation for Research in Population
Problems at Miami University conducted one such survey
in collaboration with Nanking University. Professor Ta Chen
carried out a census and vital registration for a small area
in the Kunming Lake Region in 1942. There have been other
small *ad hoc* investigations.

Various birth and death rates were deduced from these experimental studies. Before the end of World War II, the national crude birth rate for China was generally taken as forty per 1,000. The figures ranged regionally from thirty-six to about fifty per 1,000.

When the Communists came to power in 1949, they, too, initially had recourse to the conventional but unscientific figures bequeathed by the Kuomintang regime. But in the wake of the 1953 census, vital registration has been organized on a national basis. An official has been made responsible in every village to register all births and deaths. These figures are now collected annually for the whole country.

The organization of vital registration for the entire nation is a tremendous undertaking when we recall that the previous governments could not manage it for even a much smaller area. I discussed this question with a member of the National Statistical Bureau and another expert belonging to the Institute of Economic Research, both in Peking. I was told that the vital registration in rural areas was carried out at the *hsiang* level and that it was the responsibility of the People's Council of combined villages. The population of this unit is usually around a few thousands.

At the town and city level (*chungsu*), vital registration is the responsibility of the police. The parents or a responsible member of the family or the neighbors have to report a vital occurrence to the police. All this is demanded by the Vital Registration Law passed in January, 1952, by the Standing Committee of the National People's Congress. Every birth has to be registered if only for cloth and food. The officials assured me that there was today nearly 100 per cent registration. They conceded that there might be a few omissions in the border areas, but otherwise very few births and deaths went unrecorded.

At the end of every year, the *hsiang* submits a statistical report of births, deaths, immigrants, and emigrants in the area—this report goes to the county, and from there to the provincial level and finally to the center in Peking.

There is, of course, no way of checking the accuracy of vital registration all over the country. But knowing, as we do, that the Street Committees take care of everything in China, I am certain that nothing escapes the authorities. When even a minor private domestic disagreement between a husband and wife comes to the knowledge of the all-pervasive Communist Party, it would be difficult for such important events as births and deaths to escape the knowledge of the authorities.

Since the vital statistics are not published for the use of the general public, there is no easy way of obtaining them. In most countries, one can buy the Annual Report of the Registrar-General and obtain all the official vital statistics one wants. However, I asked the government for these figures, and they were supplied to me as follows:

Year	Birth Rate	Death Rate	Natural Increase
(Per 1,000 of Population)			
1953	37	17	20
1954	37	13	24
1955	35	12.4	22.6
1956	32	11.4	20.6
1957	34	11	23

These figures for all China show that the birth rate is not as high as is usually imagined abroad. Secondly, the death rate is unusually low and, what is more, reveals a steady decline. Are these figures reliable? One has nothing but the official figures, and I believe they indicate more or less the true demographic picture for China as a whole. The annual rate of increase was 2 per cent in 1953 and had increased to 2.3 in 1957. And I think the rate of increase will gradually go up for reasons which I shall discuss later. In other words, the net annual addition to China's population has been growing from 12,000,000 to 15,000,000. The annual addition may soon increase to about 20,000,000. In the years since the 1953 census, her population has already increased by a total of more than 10 per cent. It is already nearing 700,000,000.

The infant mortality rate, which is a highly sensitive index of a community's health and cultural conditions, reveals the same declining trend. In 1954, for the urban areas, it was forty-seven per 1,000 live births. In 1955, the number declined to forty-two. In 1956, it decreased further to thirty-five, a figure closer to European than Asian countries.

As for rural areas, the infant mortality rate was 138 per 1,000 live births in 1954. In 1956, it declined to 109. These figures reveal again what I believe to be the true state of affairs. (In China, a community with a population of less than 2,000 is classed as rural. Areas where more than 50 per cent of the population are peasants are also so classed.)

What are the various social and economic factors that will affect and further influence the birth and death rates in China?

Let us consider the death rate first. China, in the past, has had no regular and nation-wide health or medical services. Throughout her history, epidemics have been as regular as famines. Now the picture is fast changing for the better. Sanitation and environmental hygiene are being promoted with fervor.

Most urban communities in the past had neither underground drainage, nor protected water supply, nor proper conservancy arrangements. Now, while proper conservancy is still a problem in small towns, underground drainage and protected supply of water are being planned on a scientific basis for major towns and cities.

To these measures must be added national efforts to improve public health. Rats, dogs, flies, and mosquitoes are being eliminated on a national scale. Indiscriminate spitting receives a prompt reproof. Garbage removal and disposal are gradually coming under control.

What about medical services? Figures of the total number of hospitals, clinics, and qualified doctors for the nation as a whole are not available. Therefore, it is difficult to compare China's position in this respect (in terms of a ratio of medical personnel to units of population numbers) with other Asian or with Western countries. The Communist authorities have, however, admitted that it will take some decades before they can train an adequate number of doctors in Western medicine to meet the demands of the 700,000,000 people. So they have now embarked on a program of utilizing the services of the traditional "doctors." China has a traditional system of medicine like India's Ayurveda, Unani, and Siddha systems. But it had been looked down upon through the centuries as so much quackery, and only the Allopathic system was officially recognized and encouraged. However, the traditional doctors and herbalists, who had no academic training, continued to flourish in the countryside, catering to the needs of the rural population, which had neither Western-trained doctors nor hospitals of any kind.

Now the Communists have effectively drawn China's traditional doctors into the national picture. This has served two purposes. As part of the country's cultural renaissance, the Chinese are being taught to look upon certain aspects of their past as a glorious heritage, and not to look down upon their *vaidyas* as quacks. The Vice-Minister of Health, Mr. Wu Yun-fu, told me at the Ministry of Health, in Peking, that, though traditional Chinese medicine had been pooh-poohed in the past, it had never been given a proper scientific trial. Now every hospital—and all hospitals are, of course, run by the government—has on its staff traditional doctors on an equal footing with their Allopathic counterparts. All hospitals are carrying on research in ancient

Chinese remedies—roots, leaves, and herbs. The country's old system of acupuncture has now come into its own. In every hospital there are two departments, one Allopathic and the other traditional. And the patient can choose whichever he likes. When he does not wish to make a choice, doctors in both systems jointly examine him, diagnose, and decide on the best cure. The chances are that the traditional system is plumped for more often. This approach satisfies their intense nationalist spirit.

The second reason, which is equally if not more valid for the present situation, is that the traditional Chinese system of medicine is infinitely cheaper than the Allopathic. It does not require five to six years of intensive training for one to attain a level comparable to our M.B., B.S., or M.D., nor does it depend upon expensive imported drugs. The traditional doctors are recruited from the countryside, from families which have been practicing medicine on a hereditary basis. They are given a few months' formal training and pressed into the nation's medical services.

I visited a few medical colleges. One of them, the Sun Yat-sen Medical College at Canton, was a small medical school before the Liberation, and graduated fifty doctors annually. But today the institution has grown enormously and has on the rolls some 2,100 students. Formerly, the entire college occupied one building; as I went around with the American-educated dean, Dr. S. K. Chow, I counted eight big buildings. The attached hospital had some 850 beds. The students go to classes in three shifts. I visited a classroom where a lecture in obstetrics was in progress, and, while the professor was speaking in Chinese, I noted that the students were using a Russian textbook. "A new feature of our medical education," observed Dr. Chow, "is that our medical students must spend at least one month every year in the villages, learning and practicing among the common people. Our doctors are no longer only at the disposal of rich patients who can afford to pay a fee. And, when our students graduate, they will be posted to areas where there is great need for doctors."

In Harbin, I went around the Medical College of the Heilungkiang University. The college and hospital occupy some twenty new five- and six-storied buildings. Approximately 2,600 students are undergoing the new five-year training course of integrated Western and Chinese medicine. The two attached teaching hospitals have 1,400 beds. These new buildings were started after the Liberation and were completed in 1955.

In Peking, I visited two institutions, the hospital of the Peking Union Medical College, which is now called the Hospital of the Chinese Academy of Medical Sciences, and the Peking Children's Hospital, which was founded after the Liberation. Dr. Wu Jui-ping, Director and Pediatrician of the Children's Hospital, told me that there had been virtually no pediatric care before the Communists came to power. He pointed out that, as a result of this new Children's Hospital and the new Midwifery Service, the infant mortality rate in Peking city, which was 117 per 1,000 live births before the Liberation (comparable to India's 115 in 1955) had been brought down to 34.1 in 1957. The same was the case with maternal mortality. Before 1949, it was seven per 1,000 deliveries, but in 1957 the figure had been reduced to three.

At Wuhan, the lady director of the Number Two medical college related a similar story of how her institution had grown enormously since the Liberation. She assured me that the people in the region received adequate medical care and that, too, without any class bias.

All these factors—better and more sanitary and hygienic facilities, underground sewerage and modern methods of garbage disposal and conservancy, more and better-equipped general hospitals, maternity homes and children's hospitals—will surely have one result, that of effectively bringing down the general death rate and its components of infant and maternal mortality rates.

III

What about marriage in China? And what are the present trend in her birth rate and the factors likely to affect it in the years ahead? Before the Communists came into power, the universality of the married state had been a well-known feature of the Chinese scene. So had been the institution of concubinage. The latter, which amounted in practice to polygamy, was abolished with no great effort, and monogamy has become the law of the land.

As for marriage, the institution has become even more universal under the Communists than it was before. A Chinese sociologist in Shanghai explained to me that, in the past, economic insecurity was the only barrier to matrimony. There was always the fear that one might not be able to provide a home for a wife and the children that would arrive. But, under Communism, there is no fear of unemployment or inadequate wages, for it is now the State's responsibility to provide jobs and the necessities of life for all the children one may want to have. The economic deterrent to marriage or the factors responsible for its postponement no longer exist. Besides, professional prostitution has been abolished, and those women with liberal morals who are to be found in most societies are no longer in evidence. Therefore, all eligible young men and women get married.

The reform of the Chinese marriage law was one of the first things that received attention from the new regime. As early as November 7, 1931, the constitution of the Chinese Soviet Republic was proclaimed by Mao Tse-tung, Chairman of the Provisional Government of the Soviet Republic of China, at the first All-China Congress of Soviets held in Juichin, Kiangsi province. The marriage reform provisions of this paper constitution were embodied in Article II, which reads: "The Chinese Soviet Government guarantees the emancipation of women; it recognizes the freedom of marriage, and puts into operation measures defending women, enabling them gradually to attain the material basis required for their emancipation from the slavery of domestic work and for participation in the social, economic, and political life of the country."

The Communists were true to their promise. In April, 1950, that is, soon after the Liberation, the Central People's Government promulgated the New Marriage Law. This law has numerous provisions, but only a few can be referred to here.

Marriage for the first time in the nation's long history has been made a civil contract and not a religious ceremony. Secondly, it has to be registered, which is the condition of legitimacy. The procedure is defined as follows: "For the registration of marriage: first, both parties, the man and the woman, shall go in person either to the man's or the woman's city, village, etc., of residence to fill in the application form at the registry. After the application form is filled, bring it to the police station to get it endorsed. After that, both parties shall each take the Pre-nuptial Health Examination form to the appointed hospital for examination. If there is no physiological defect or disease, if all the procedures mentioned are complied with, and if they are proved in conformity with [other articles] of the law, registration may be granted. Moreover, they are subject to the approval of the local People's Government before marriage certificates are obtainable."

A desirable feature of this directive is the compulsory, pre-marital medical examination of the prospective couple. But the permits by the police and the local People's Government may involve bureaucratic delays unless the bride and groom are acceptable to the Party. Another welcome feature is embodied in Article 4, which raises the age of consent from eighteen to twenty for males and from sixteen to eighteen for females.

As for the rights and duties of husband and wife, Article 8 stipulates: "Husband and wife are in duty bound to love, respect, assist and look after each other, to live in harmony, to labor for production, to care for the children, to strive jointly for the welfare of the family and the building up of a new society."

In brief, all the fetters on individual freedom of marriage have been removed. Marriages based on arbitrary and compulsory arrangements by parents or senior members of the family as well as those by purchase or gifts are no longer permitted. The wife can use her maiden name or her previous married name or the name of her present husband. The social barriers against a widow's remarriage have been removed, and divorce has been made relatively easy. Children born out of wedlock have the same rights as legitimate children. All these reforms had been discussed by the KMT groups for many years, but it was left to the Communists to bring in legislation incorporating these provisions and, what is more important (unlike India's Sarda Act), enforce them. Thus the Chinese marriage law has been brought up to date and in consonance with practice in advanced Communist countries like the Soviet Union.

What is likely to be the effect of the new law on the country's population problem? I believe it will be to help increase China's population. The marriage rate is higher now, and so is the birth rate.

The growth of population in any country is conditioned by three factors—births, deaths, and migration. Emigration from China today is completely absent (except for the seepage via Hong Kong and Macao). If anything, there is immigration from the Chinese overseas settlements. In fact, the Communist government is doing all it can to attract the overseas Chinese and is building some overseas Chinese villages—modern suburban communities. The reasons behind this are intriguing and will be discussed in a later section. For the present, China has no emigration outlets, nor is she seeking any at present.

Her growth of population will, therefore, be conditioned by the balance between births and deaths. Some of the major factors which affect the death rate and which are responsible for its gradual but definite decline have already been referred to. Every effort is being made to bring down infant, child, maternal, and over-all mortality rates. The great epidemics which once ravaged the countryside have lost their terrors. Floods and famines are under control, thanks to water conservancy and greater agricultural production. With better sanitation and hygiene, protected water supply, and better conservancy measures, the rate of disease in China, as a whole, according to all the available evidence, has come down. Along with this, as pointed out earlier, the death rate has also declined in recent years. And if the official death rates are accepted, one can say that China may soon reach the low level registered by some advanced European nations.

With near-universal marriages and the current social attitudes that favor large numbers for their own sake and treat any talk of population pressure as neo-Malthusian nonsense, and with the absence of any widespread practice of contraception, the birth rate is bound to remain as high as it is now. It is obvious that the survival rate is high and will progressively increase, other things remaining the same. And at the present rate of increase, China's population in 1963—the end of her second Five-Year Plan—will be about 700,000,000. It will be 800,000,000 before 1968, the end of her third Five-Year Plan.

Can China feed, clothe, house, and provide the necessary social services for her increasing numbers? Can her agricultural and industrial production and her plans for internal migration take care of the numerous problems posed by this alarming growth? Or will she be forced to embark on a national family-planning policy? What is her population policy, if any?

Generally, a country's demographic, economic, and social facts lead to what is called a population problem. It may be one of too many or too few numbers. And the governments may embark on a population policy to meet such a problem. But in totalitarian countries, it is the other way around. The socio-economic situation leads to a problem, and the policy adopted by the government aggravates it in terms of the land-man as well as the population-resources ratios. Such a situation eventually leads to open or latent demands on other nations. And the ultimate outcome is war.

But China did embark upon a vigorous and nation-wide policy to promote birth control in 1957. The circumstances that led to the decision to launch a family-planning campaign, including the great debate on Marxist versus Malthusian views of China's population problem, the reasons for the particular decision, the vigor with which it was executed, and the factors that compelled the sudden withdrawal of the family-planning campaign and a reversal of the entire nation's propaganda machine in favor of a large population, the attacks and recriminations (a kind of ideological civil war) between those favoring population control and those against, the hair-splitting, unrealistic, Marxist theoretical controversy—all this makes a fascinating story. It also reveals the mental moorings of Marxist theorists and the inner contradictions of totalitarian thinking.

IV

The first session of the People's Congress, held in Peking in September, 1954, witnessed the beginning of the great debate on China's population problems and on the need for birth control. It was Deputy Shao Li-tzu who first publicly raised the issue of birth control before the Congress and set the ball rolling.

(Since even the so-called public debates on national questions are usually started with the Party's permission, it is
reasonable to infer that the government—and the Party
which runs the government—felt the need to disseminate
information on birth control for a variety of reasons. The
major reason was the unsatisfactory food situation in 1954,
bordering on quasi-famine in a few provinces, and the lack
of housing and hospital facilities for the growing population.)

In his speech, Shao Li-tzu made it quite clear that there
was no population problem in China in the conventional,
bourgeois, capitalistic sense, and his plea for birth control
had nothing to do with decadent, outmoded, and reactionary
Malthusian doctrines. His plea for introducing birth-control
measures was based on the need for protecting and improving
the health of hard-working Chinese mothers and affording
better opportunities for their children. "A big population,"
he pointed out, "is a good thing, but there should be a
certain limit to it when there are many difficulties." This
cautious government-approved statement was followed by
speeches by several other Deputies on more or less the same
lines as Deputy Shao's. As a result of this debate, the State
Council issued a firm directive to the Ministry of Health
to educate the masses on the need for practicing birth control—both "contraception and artificial expulsion" (scientific
contraception as well as induced abortion).

On December 27, 1954, Liu Shao-chi, one of the big five
in China, next only to Mao Tse-tung and considered a
great Marxist theorist, convened a conference to discuss the
problems relating to birth control. The association of Liu
Shao-chi with birth control at that moment revealed to the
people how serious and earnest the government was on
the question. As a result of this conference, the Second
General Office of the State Council "designated the responsible officials of the competent departments to organize research groups for the discussion of contraception problems."

Now the whole nation had received the green light on birth control, and every meeting of the Party at the village, town, and State level began to discuss the advantages of birth control for China. •In the summer of 1955, Premier Chou En-lai, speaking on behalf of the Central Committee of the Communist Party on "Measures Relative to the Development of the National Economy and the Second Five-Year Plan," pleaded for "appropriate control in respect of births." This declaration firmly put the official seal on a nation-wide campaign for birth control.

(However, it may be recalled that in early 1955, when Mr. Nehru visited Peking, Chou En-lai scoffed at the idea of population control. He reminded Mr. Nehru of China's vast territory in the north and middle west capable of absorbing millions of surplus people.)

All over the country governmental and Party groups were set up to study, conduct research on, and advocate birth control. This period of intellectual incubation was necessary to answer orthodox Communist theorists on the Marxian aspect of birth control and to accumulate the experience and knowledge gained on the subject by countries such as India on the one hand and the Soviet Union on the other. When Premier Chou En-lai visited India in November, 1956, one of his first requests in New Delhi was for information on India's experience in family-planning.

Throughout 1957, Peking waged a determined campaign, as only Peking can, for birth control. Madam Li Ten-chuan, Minister for Health, in the course of her report before the National People's Congress in March, 1957, said: "We have not employed enough propaganda on the question of birth control which affects the health of women and children, the education of children, and the prosperity of the nation." She pleaded for further dedicated efforts toward propaganda and education and stressed the need for technical guidance.

Madam Li was specific and emphatic in her appeal for nation-wide adoption of birth control. She said: "Our country is a big and overpopulated one, and in the course of our socialistic construction various undertakings are being developed in a planned manner. If our population growth is not in accordance with planned childbirth, it will prevent our country from quickly ridding itself of poverty and from becoming prosperous and powerful. For instance, taking the rate of growth at 2.5 per cent, there will be an increase of 15,000,000 every year, and our population will reach over 700,000,000 in the Second Five-Year Plan period (1958-1962). Actually, owing to the development of medical and public health work and to the improvement of living conditions, the rate of natural increase will be more than 2.5 per cent. . . . With such a huge rate of growth, the increase of our agricultural and industrial production, however rapid, will fail to satisfy adequately the basic requirements of the increased population."

On March 5, 1958, the *People's Daily* carried an editorial entitled "Exercise Appropriate Birth Control," pleading for birth control and pointing out that the necessary organization for implementing the program had been set up and that the contraceptives necessary were available. It pointed out that there was a great need for birth control "to fight a fast-increasing population, especially in the rural areas. China is the world's most populous country and, at 2.2 per cent, the increase is the highest annual rate of growth. However, industrial production has been increasing at 10 per cent and agricultural output at 5 per cent, which is higher than the increase in population. But, if the speed of our population slows down, improvement in the livelihood of our people will quicken correspondingly. Therefore, we advocate that, except for the sparsely populated minorities zones, all areas in our country must promote appropriate birth control."

Now things began to move at a rapid pace. On March 7, 1958, the Health Minister, in her report to the nation, spoke on "the question of contraception for which all of you have shown general concern." She revealed that, during 1957, active propaganda through lectures and pamphlets, slides and films, stationary and peripatetic exhibitions on contraception had been organized on a near-national scale. Reviewing the results, she asked for closer cooperation between the various government departments, health units, trade unions, and youth leagues, and appealed for their active support in carrying out the birth-control campaign successfully to make family-planning a part of the people's mores.

On August 6, 1958, the Ministry of Health issued directives to all the health departments in the provinces, autonomous regions and districts and municipalities on the "need for leading the great masses to plan births and control the spacing of pregnancies."

Between September, 1958, and May, 1959 (when suddenly the birth-control campaign was called off, for reasons which will be explored later), the country witnessed a sustained campaign to popularize birth control all over the country and at all levels.

"An ideal family," pointed out the newspapers, "should have three or four children, in a planned manner; the first child should be two or three years older than the second, the second four to six years older than the third, and the third two or three years older than the fourth."

Family-planning exhibitions and technical guidance centers were opened in many Chinese towns and villages to explain the official policy of population control. Newspaper and magazine articles, radio talks, stationary and traveling exhibitions, official instructions and singing guides were pressed into service all over the country to hammer away on the need for limiting the size of families, the advantages to be derived from doing so, and the means of effecting it.

When I visited China, the policy of population control had been reversed, and all the birth-control exhibitions had been closed down. But I tracked down the newspaper records and comments of visiting foreigners on these exhibitions. According to one foreign observer: "Exhibitions in all the major cities show pictures of harassed parents surrounded by anything up to a dozen squalling children, burdened to death by troublesome brats, and unable to get on with their work or enjoy their leisure. These exhibitions are also taken around the innumerable villages. In contrast, other pictures show the tranquil happiness enjoyed by parents who have four or even less children.

"A small family, it is proclaimed to those who visit the exhibitions, allows father to get on with his work in the evening or frees mother to go to the factory during the day. This is a revolution in Chinese thinking hardly less great than any that China has yet undergone. For nearly 3,000 years, all Chinese have been taught to venerate the large family, and have had instilled into them the virtue of many descendants to worship their family ancestors. Now they are told the exact opposite."

The observer continues: "The exhibitions I visited in two of China's principal cities, Peking and Canton, were well attended, though I visited both on working days. Both displayed long series of drawings, showing the vertiginous figures of the increase in the Chinese birth rate, the happy home with the small family, and the exact method of arriving at this desired result. Forbidding-looking female guides lectured to little parties of visitors in front of each exhibit."

The realism of the diagrams in these exhibitions was almost shocking to many a visiting moralist, though it was difficult to ascertain the reactions of the Chinese men and women. Complete and intimate details were shown in what amounted to almost animated diagrams; and anything which was not clear was explained by the women guides without any prudery or squeamishness.

The wife of one of our embassy officials in Peking told me that she visited the Birth-Control Exhibition in Peking, but she was so embarrassed at the intimate exhibits being viewed jointly by men and women that she promptly returned home. When I asked an Indian lady student at Peking University—a young mother—about the exhibition, she replied that she had gone all through it, but added: "An exhibition like that wouldn't last for a day in our country."

This stark realism, which left nothing to the imagination, had a simple objective. The authorities were not leaving anything to chance. Even the most illiterate peasant and the least intelligent worker went away from the exhibition knowing exactly what to do to prevent conception.

The Ministry of Health also produced an excellent film in the Chinese language (shot in Shanghai) on "Control of Conception." It was shown not only in every theater all over the country, but to various groups in the countryside. This film, which shows all the available means of family-planning, is now withdrawn, and it was after repeated requests that the Ministry of Health consented to show it to me privately at their offices. My only companions at this film show were the Vice-Minister of Health and my interpreter. I asked permission to buy a print of the film but was refused on the ground that export of the film, even to a friendly country like India, might give people a misleading and wrong impression that China had a population problem and that the Communist economy could not cope with it.

Throughout the campaign the authorities directed their attack along the following four lines, in order of importance: contraception, late marriages, induced or clinical abortion, and sterilization for either partner. The legal minimum age for marriage under the Chinese Marriage Law, as already pointed out, is at present eighteen for women and twenty for men. The Chinese National People's Congress considered a number of proposals for raising the age of consent by several years.

How was the movement received by the public, especially the mothers? I cannot do better than quote what Dr. Chou

Ngo-feu of the Bureau of Women's and Children's Health at the Ministry of Health says: "The majority of the Chinese people have no knowledge of birth control. The fact of the matter is that many people know very little about physiology and hygiene. Another stumbling block in the work of popularizing birth control is the fact that many people are still influenced by the old feudal ways of thought. They still consider conception and birth as a completely mysterious process and, indeed, feel that even the mention of it is taboo. It requires both patience and tact to persuade such people to accept the modern views.

"Our work of popularizing birth control began in 1955, and ever since that time the newspapers and magazines have had articles on the subject constantly. The government departments concerned have issued pamphlets and posters, used lantern slides, held exhibitions, meetings, and lectures to spread the knowledge of birth control. The aim is to explain both the technique and significance of birth control, to show that it is a matter which concerns both husband and wife and that both must cooperate for successful family-planning, and to strike a blow at feudal and obscurantist ideas. The various contraceptive methods and devices are explained, and people are told where they can be bought and what places to go to or get in touch with for advice. All this has met with a warm welcome from the public. The Ministry of Health ran one meeting on contraception which they intended to be quite a small affair and printed only 700 tickets, and 2,000 people turned up! An exhibition on contraceptive methods in Yutien county in Hopei drew 50,000 visitors during the week it was on."

V

It is not known who was primarily responsible for calling off the intensive nation-wide campaign for birth control in China, or at what level the decision was reached. Anyway, the stationary and peripatetic exhibitions on family-planning were closed down, and the educational campaign to reduce the nation's birth rate was turned off just as it was gathering momentum. A week earlier, it had been patriotic and proper for a comrade citizen to plan and limit the size of his family, and by the next week talk of overpopulation had become bourgeois, Malthusian, and reactionary!

Several explanations have been advanced by foreign observers for this sudden reversal of policy. (Consistency has never been a conspicuous virtue with Communism. The most blatant change in Communist policy in another realm was witnessed during World War II. The war had been branded by the Communists as imperialist, leaving no choice between Hitler, who was fighting for an empire, and the Allies—Britain and France—who already had their own empires. But the *Imperialist War* suddenly became a *People's War* the day the Führer launched his attack against the Soviet Union!) The Chinese themselves have never explained why their birth-control policy was reversed, but the most plausible explanation according to many observers is that a sudden shift in population policy became necessary because the impression had gained ground that the nation-wide birth-control drive implied that Peking was incapable of delivering the goods. It invited, in other words, a vote of no confidence in Communism. It is surmised, therefore, that in order to bolster complete confidence in the economy and persuade the people that a heaven on earth could be constructed within decades, Peking decided to abandon the 1957 campaign to control fertility and revert to the *laissez-faire* policy of allowing the *status quo* of an increasing population to continue.

One of the major contributors to the population debate in China was Dr. Ma Yin-chu. His rise and fall, his contribution, and his subsequent denunciation constitute an intriguing episode in all the discussions pertaining to China's population problems.

On July 3, 1957, Dr. Ma Yin-chu, an economist and scholar of some repute and President of Peking University, delivered a written statement before the fourth session of the First National People's Congress of China on "A New Theory of Population." At first, the speech presenting this paper was apparently ignored, or, at any rate, it received no particular comment, and the author continued to enjoy his scholarly reputation as well as his academic position.

Recently, however, there has been a widespread and virulent attack on Dr. Ma for the view expressed in his paper—in November and December, 1958. Articles appearing in various newspapers and periodicals (all newspapers are officially controlled, of course) denounced him as a Malthusian and a rightist. Daily newspapers, political and economic periodicals, women's magazines, and trade union journals all joined in the fray. The Doctor had little chance to reply or to explain his theory, and the upshot of the attack was that he was asked to resign from the presidency of the university.

I asked many university men and others what the offending demographic thesis was. No one could outline or explain the essay, but all were unanimous in their denunciation of Dr. Ma as a sneaky Malthusian and a rightist. Apparently Dr. Ma's predicament was very much like that of Thomas Robert Malthus in his time: nobody had read him but everybody attacked him. And in Dr. Ma's case, denunciation was the official line.

I expressed a desire, through my host organization, to meet the Doctor. After a few days, I was told that he had gone away to the countryside and was at a camp for the rectification of "rightist intellectuals." But I gathered from a foreign embassy that Dr. Ma was, in fact, still in Peking. I repeated my request and wondered whether I could be permitted to go to the countryside to meet him, as I was particularly interested in population theories. I was told by my interpreter that Dr. Ma was quite an old man, "beyond seventy," that I would not find him stimulating, and that it would not be worth my trouble. A few days later I again raised the question of my meeting Dr. Ma. I now received a final, definite answer that I could not meet him because Dr. Ma was "on compulsory medical leave!" (I must add here that in Communist China—and I believe in other totalitarian countries as well—a foreign visitor cannot just phone or write or call on anyone he likes without official approval, because doing so would embarrass or otherwise cause trouble for the person concerned. This seems like a small and insignificant freedom—until it is lost.)

What did Dr. Ma write? What was his *New Theory* of *Population?* I have now carefully read his paper in an English translation (it runs to some thirty pages), and I am unable to find anything dreadful or reactionary either in his central theme or in his reasoning about China's population problem. This is not the place to enter into any learned or technical discussion on the thesis. I may, however, briefly summarize it in his own language:

"China will find it extremely difficult to achieve lasting prosperity unless her population growth is severely curbed. The annual rate of growth is assumed to be 2 per cent. But it is probably much higher than 2 per cent because the number of marriages has been on the increase. Before the Liberation, we had an enormous unemployment problem, and this was a deterrent to marriage and to starting a new family. Now everyone on leaving school is assigned to some work, and therefore he or she promptly gets married and starts a new family. No one now has to give any assistance to one's old father, brothers, or relatives as before, because the government is taking care of old people and other former family obligations. . . .

"Secondly, thanks to better health service, maternal mortality and the death rate among old people are coming down. Following the change in the social system, most of the monks and nuns (in the Catholic and other orders) have returned to the laity and got married, and in the future very few people will become monks or nuns. Prostitutes have been rehabilitated, and they are getting married and starting their own families. In view of these and other factors, death rates have been lowered and the birth rate is going up. The annual rate of growth is much more than the assumed 2 per cent. . . .

"The capital accumulation is not rapid enough in China. Since population is huge and net annual additions are large, capital accumulation is small. Though production has increased, national consumption has also increased. The way to increase capital formation is not to cut down consumption but to cut down the number of people. Hence I advocate strict population control. . . .

"As we all know, Malthus' principle of population is reactionary. His principle of population was practically one of telling the workers that their prevalent poverty was not the fault of the government but mainly due to the too rapid increase of population and the too slow increase in food. It was exactly on this point that he was fundamentally wrong." (Dr. Ma Yin-chu, like a good Communist, took sufficient care to attack Malthus, but this was of no avail to him after all.)

"My principle of population is different in stand from Malthus'. I believe that the more developed the socialist enterprises are, the more expanded will mechanization and automation become. A thing which formerly required 1,000 persons to accomplish will require only fifty persons. Then, may I ask, what are we going to do with the 950 persons? For this reason I am worried that, with more people, we cannot become mechanized and automatized at a high speed. One of the reasons for our inability to build any large-size industries and for the necessity of our building more small- and medium-size industries is because small- and medium-size industries can take in more workers. But, since our country is heading toward socialism, we should build a large number of large-size industries. Lenin also said that, without large-size industries, there can be no socialism. However, since our population is too large, it drags down the speed of industrialization and prevents us from taking big strides forward. Some people call me a Malthusian; yet I call these people dogmatists and anti-Leninists.

"Among the 13,000,000-increase this year, only 1,000,000 can find jobs in industries, while the other 12,000,000 will have to work in the countryside. But nowadays each peasant can create a wealth of at most some eighty *yuan* for the State each year, while a worker in a factory, because of modern technical equipment, can create a wealth of over 4,000 *yuan* for the State each year. The ratio of these two is 1 to 50. The principal reason for such a huge difference between these two rates of productivity is that industrial production can make use of modern technical equipment while agricultural production can only use draft animals as the main motive power. Besides, in some provinces there recently appeared the phenomenon of using man-power to pull the plow because many draft animals had died and many of the living ones were lean and weak, thus still more adversely affecting agricultural production. . . .

"We will not condescend to ask for loans from the United States, nor can we use the method of imperialist exploitation of colonies to squeeze capital from the people, nor can we imitate Japan in using the indemnity she got from China after the Sino-Japanese War of 1894 as capital for her industrialization. What we can do is to depend on our own strength and our own accumulation [capital formation]. But the ratio between our own accumulation and consumption is 21 per cent to 79 per cent. Can we reduce our consumption a little and also increase our accumulation a little? Judging by the actual conditions in our country, this is rather dangerous. . . .

"Our national income is rather small and is divided into

two parts, accumulation and consumption. If accumulation increases, consumption invariably decreases, and then it will be unavoidable that the people's livelihood will not be sufficiently taken care of. On the other hand, if consumption increases, accumulation invariably decreases, in which case the completion of industrialization will inevitably be delayed. Hence a balance must necessarily be reached between the two. As to how to reach this balance, actual conditions should be taken into consideration. . . .

"In the Soviet Union, consumption occupies 75 per cent while accumulation represents 25 per cent—or one-fourth of the national income. In China, since the people's living standards are comparatively low and the population is comparatively large, it is only natural for consumption to occupy a relatively higher percentage and, therefore, we have the ratio of 79 per cent to 21 per cent. We cannot follow the example of the Soviet Union by raising the accumulation to 25 per cent and suppressing the consumption to 75 per cent. If we do this, it means that we care only about industrialization and not about the people. Then trouble will be unavoidable.

"One of the reasons for the Polish and Hungarian incidents is precisely that the government paid attention only to industrialization and not to the needs of the people, changing the people's zeal for industrialization into disappointment in life, and thus causing trouble. We now settle the annual increase of some 12,000,000 surplus people in rural areas; though we have no other alternative, yet side effects are unavoidable. Nowadays, peasants always want to keep a little more of the grain they produce, and to catch up gradually with the standard of urban inhabitants in respect to livelihood requirements. They want to have more edible oil, and thus the supply of edible oil is more limited than that of grain. They want to wear more new clothes, and thus cloth is in shortage (of course, the shortage of cotton is also one of the reasons) and cloth tickets can fetch only half of their denoted quantity. Therefore, while the 12,000,000 newly increased population whom we settle in rural areas every year cannot raise their labor productivity within a short period, they nevertheless try to catch up with urban people in respect to their living requirements. If such a situation should last long, how dangerous the outcome would be!

"For this reason, if we do not try to solve the population problem at an early date, sooner or later the peasants will change all the favors and kindness they have received into feelings of despair and discontent; and though the result may not be the same as what happened in Poland and Hungary, it inevitably will bring a lot of headaches for the government. Hence I advocate the elevation of peasants' labor productivity, accumulating capital on the one hand, and controlling population on the other. Otherwise, we would simply make efforts in vain."

Dr. Ma goes on to add that it is necessary not only to accumulate capital but also to speed up the accumulation. And judging from the present position of the availability of industrial raw materials, it is absolutely necessary to control the growth of population. If the population is allowed to increase in its natural course without any restraint, then the speed of industrialization is bound to be affected by it. And last but not least, he says that judging from the point of view of total food supply, China is not yet out of the woods and thus there is an absolute need for population control. Finally Dr. Ma outlines various methods of population control acceptable to the Chinese masses. He concludes that, unless the nation's numbers are brought under control, no rapid industrialization and no real socialism will be possible in China.

A careful perusal of Dr. Ma's paper and his reasoning reveals a fairly elementary and acceptable analysis of China's demographic position in relation to her plans for rapid economic development. The country's economy in relation to its population problems presents all the familiar features of an underdeveloped economy trying to reconcile the slow pace of her over-all economic and social development with the rapid rate of her population increase. I must confess that I am not an expert on the devious dialectics of Marxist economic theory, but I fail to see anything reactionary in Dr. Ma's approach despite his loud disclaimer of any Malthusian bias. Under the circumstances, it is difficult to understand why this honest essay brought such a hornets' nest about the author's ears.

The official attacks against Dr. Ma have in the main been directed to show that 650,000,000 Chinese are not too many; that they are the raw material and the seminal force to build a strong, industrialized and socialist China; that while birth control is advocated, it is not because China has too many mouths to feed but solely on the grounds of the health and welfare of mothers. Tweedledum or Tweedledee!

It is difficult for a foreign observer like the present writer to see exactly where Dr. Ma overstepped the official line which resulted in his denunciation. Perhaps it was the honesty inherent in his arguments, which are free both from any political bias and from any desire to play to the gallery. It is also curious that, in essence, his arguments are the ones which the Party faithful had been parading over the months. And what is even more surprising is that Dr. Ma's major suggestion had been adopted in the main by the country. The only three reasons that I could gather indirectly from my talks with Chinese officials are that Dr. Ma had the effrontery to refer to Poland and Hungary and to suggest that People's China could ever have similar problems of discontent. Secondly, Dr. Ma's paper was considered frankly pessimistic. A note of pessimism, no matter how honest or how well-founded, has no place in the present difficult stage of this new society when nothing but the most positive optimism should permeate the people's thinking. And how can anyone dare to be pessimistic about a Communist economy with the Soviet sputniks and satellites in the sky! And the third reason would seem to be that the government had decided to reverse its line on the whole population question, and Dr. Ma merely served as a convenient scapegoat.

(A lesson to be learned from this controversy, which, however, is not relevant to the present discussion of China's population question, is that one cannot afford to be intellectually honest under Communism.)

VI

I had numerous discussions on the population question with doctors, economists, statisticians, government and Party officials wherever I went. From what I could gather, the official position today is that China is not overpopulated and that she has no population problem in quantitative terms. Every human being is primarily a producer and only secondarily a consumer. There is no greater wealth than that constituted by human beings, and there is nothing that humans cannot achieve. From the point of view of the work that is to be done and the targets yet to be achieved, 650,000,000 people are not nearly enough, and the country is really underpopulated and there is an acute labor shortage!

All this does not mean that birth-control advice or contraceptives are not available today in China. The campaign has been withdrawn purely for psychological reasons, and if birth control has no place from the economic angle, it does have a definite place from the health point of view. Professor K. P. Lin of the Department of Gynecology and Obstetrics at the Sun Yat-sen Medical College in Canton told me that today birth-control advice and appliances are available in all major hospitals and they have not been withdrawn despite the fact that the campaign in favor of birth control has been dropped. Birth control is left to the discretion of the doctors, who recommend it to harassed mothers for spacing pregnancies rather than for limitation of births, unless, of course, the health of the mother demands an end to her pregnancies—in this case post-partum sterilization is carried out with the consent of the wife and after informing the husband.

Again, Dr. Wu Jui-ping, Director of the Children's Hospital in Peking, told me that every hospital had a birth-control clinic and that the major objective of family-planning work was to protect the health of the working mother. "Unplanned pregnancies interfere with production in factories and farms, and a majority of our textile workers, for instance, are women," he added. "We now have the right to perform an abortion, if necessary, in the interest of the mother's health. We grant the abortion within eight weeks of conception. The husband, as well as the head of the institution where the woman works, must approve."

The most authoritative statement on the place of birth control was given to me by the Vice-Minister for Health, Mr. Wu Yun-fu. I asked him about China's present family-planning program, and he told me this: "There seems to be some misunderstanding on this question abroad ever since the campaign for birth control was called off at the beginning of the year. We don't call it family-planning or birth control or planned parenthood. These terms have an entirely different connotation. We in China call it *planned births.*"

"How does this term differ from other terms we use in India?" I asked.

"By planned births, we mean giving birth in a planned way."

"This looks to me like a distinction without a difference," I said.

"No, no. There is a difference. Planned births are for the sake of the mother's health. Too many births have a bad effect on work, production, and study."

By this, the Minister meant that too many pregnancies meant a woman's absence from factory or farm, and this interfered with the nation's production. Besides, too many children in a family would not leave any leisure for the mother, or, for that matter, for the father. As Communist China encourages everybody to study intensively during leisure hours, a large family is a handicap. All adults are encouraged to study two things—first, the Communist doctrine and thus get themselves properly indoctrinated to fit in mentally with the nation's plans, and, secondly, all about their own jobs, however small or trivial they may be, so that they can be expert and thus contribute to higher production. It is now an accepted doctrine that too many children in rapid succession interfere with the nation's production by requiring so many man-hours and by interfering with the necessary leisure for study.

"We don't propagate contraception, for contraception is not the end of our policy," continued the Minister. "Two births may be considered too few and six children may not be considered too many. It is an individual matter, depending upon the health of the mother, her work in the factory or on the farm, and her need to study and improve herself. The government has not laid any restriction on the number of children a couple can have; they may and should have as many children as they can, so long as the health of the mother is not impaired."

"Can a mother resort to contraception on economic grounds, that is, for reasons of poverty?" I asked.

"But there is no poverty today, thanks to our cooperatives and communes. All children are taken care of. So there is no question of poverty being a reason for controlling the size of the family," replied the Minister.

The Minister than introduced me to Madam Yang Kwang, Director of Maternal and Child Health Services in the Ministry of Health. She explained the population policy to me, more or less on the same lines as the Minister had done.

Madam Yang pointed out: "In pre-Liberation China, many

babies were born, but many babies also died. The survival rate was low. After the Liberation, the preservation of health of children and mothers was stipulated in the national program. Before the Liberation, infant and maternal mortality rates were high, and deliveries were conducted in a most unscientific way. Since the Liberation, the Ministry of Health has brought together all the traditional Chinese midwives and taught them modern and scientific methods of child delivery.

"In the last few years," she continued, "we have trained some 600,000 midwives. These are now assigned to rural areas. We are now setting up schools for the training of midwives. Graduates of junior middle schools [equivalent to the third year of high school] are given three years' training before they are posted, primarily in rural areas, as midwives. Each production team in rural areas has its own health center."

"What about urban areas?" I asked.

"The position in urban areas is easier, for we set up Maternity and Child Health Centers where expectant mothers and babies receive all the attention they need."

Then the Vice-Minister explained to me the plans for expanding medical education. He asked me whether I had visited the new medical colleges and hospitals in Harbin, Chengchow, Wuhan, or in Peking itself. I told him I had visited the large new institutions in all these cities. "Then you know what we are doing," he said. "But we have plans for further expansion," he added.

I asked about figures of medical personnel. How many doctors, dentists, and nurses does China have per 10,000 of population? The Minister did not have the latest figures, for the picture was changing daily. "But roughly we have 70,000 doctors educated in Western medicine for all China. And we have some 530,000 traditional Chinese doctors and the nurses number about 120,000. We have plans for tremendous expansion. As part of our Great Leap Forward, we are planning to double the number of our medical personnel in a few years.

"For instance," Dr. Yang pointed out, "more than 2,000,-000 creches have been set up this year to take care of 20,-000,000 babies."

"If I may change the subject, I would like to know the present official position on abortion," I said.

"We do not have at present any law for or against abortion. But abortions are permitted. When an expectant mother is seriously ill, or is suffering from some incurable disease, or if she has changed her mind for some relevant reasons, the hospital may permit an induced abortion. There is no specific set-up to take care of abortions. They are handled in the hospitals in a routine fashion on the merits of each case, with, of course, the consent of both husband and wife. For instance, I learned the other day that an opera singer going abroad on a cultural delegation was found pregnant and was granted an abortion," the Vice-Minister explained.

I then inquired about Chinese vital statistics. I wondered whether the Ministry of Health had published China's annual statistics. I received the answer that they had not. "What are your present birth and death rates, and do you have any targets for lowering these?" I asked. The Vice-Minister did not know China's birth and death rates! When I confessed my surprise that the Ministry of Health did not have any figures on the country's vital statistics, the Minister was a little upset, and my interpreter felt annoyed.

Weeks later, by the conclusion of my trip, I understood that in Communist China each department is encouraged to know all about its business and not ask a thing about any other department, no matter how closely the activities may be interrelated. For instance, an official in the Ministry of Trade knows all about his business and does not know, or is not allowed to know, anything about what is going on in another ministry—for example, the Ministry of Production! It was incredible that a Minister in the Ministry of Health should not have any idea of the nation's vital statistics with which the Ministry's activities are so intimately bound up. It is considered unnecessary for a member of the Department of Health to know the ideas of the Medical Department on a particular question. And yet somewhere, at some mysterious level near the top, there is obviously near-perfect coordination. Otherwise, of course, nothing would get done.

(I observed this water-tight compartmental approach in other matters also. For instance, when two Russian delegations are staying in a hotel, it is very seldom that a member of one delegation will communicate with any member of the other delegation. When one foreign Communist meets another of the same nationality, even if they are Russians, they cut each other dead, for one does not know the other's errand, and it is better to keep out of trouble. Further, one cannot be sure who is watching and what the report on such an accidental meeting and exchange is likely to be!)

As already observed, while the vigorous campaign for birth control had been called off, family-planning services in hospitals and clinics were still available. I learned that, during the birth-control campaign period, four contraceptive factories were opened, with partial Soviet technical aid, in Tientsin, Peking, Canton, and Shanghai. But the first two were closed down when I was in China.

In conclusion, what is likely to be the result of this meandering population policy? The welcome vigorous policy in promoting public health, provision of free medicine, maternal and child health services, and other allied measures is contributing to a gradual but definitive decline in the death rates of all age groups. The ambivalent birth-control policy is not helping to reduce the present high birth rate. Even if the present birth rate is not raised, it is sufficiently high to yield a large survival rate, thanks to the declining death rate. When this result is examined in the light of China's youthful age composition and the sex ratio, the potentialities for the future growth of her population are enormous—

granting, of course, that other factors like political stability and international peace remain the same. Under certain assumptions of stationary or rising fertility and declining mortality and the near universality of the married state, certain projections of China's population growth can be made for the next few decades. It is obvious, without going into precise, mathematical calculations, that the population is bound to increase annually by about 20,000,000 in the next few years. And the rate of growth itself will gradually increase.

Can China have a billion people by 1980? Possible or probable? It is rash to prophesy. Granting that this number is possible and probable, the question one might ask is what does it portend, for China's own economy, for the security of Southeast Asia, for peace in Asia, and for the free world? These are difficult but necessary questions that a student of international affairs must face sooner or later. Can China clothe, feed, house, and generally take care of her millions? Will she dump her commodities and services or export human beings? Has she any emigration outlets? Will Russia or the free world provide any outlets? If not, will China become a demographic danger spot and explode in quest of *Lebensraum?*

VII

From what has been said earlier about China's census figures and her annual vital statistics, it is possible to foresee that the net annual addition to her population within a decade may become some 20,000,000. That is, under certain conditions, after 1970 or so, China is likely to add to her population in *one decade* more than the present population of the United States of America. And this formidable decennial addition will gradually grow, for it is rather difficult for population numbers to become stabilized at any particular figure in a totalitarian country that has no national policy of restricting its birth rate. It is possible, if not probable, for China to have within her frontiers a billion people around

1980, if her death rate continues to decline and her birth
rate remains even stationary. Thus her population may increase as indicated below:

1953	583,000,000
1956	630,000,000
1961	700,000,000
1966	770,000,000
1971	850,000,000
1976	930,000,000
1981	1,000,000,000 or more

At the current rate of growth of 2 per cent (which itself
will increase to 2.5 or even 3 per cent possibly within a decade), China will double her population in the next twenty-
five years. Peace, rapid industrialization, the increase in total
national income, the growth of necessary social services and
modern methods of disease control through public health
engineering, medical services, and a gradual rise in the levels
of living—all are conducive to a growth in numbers.

But mere numbers mean nothing. They must be examined
in terms of the available land area—habitable, cultivable, or
otherwise exploitable—other resources, the size of the labor
force, and the stage of technological development of the
country. Theoretically, no nation need lament the fact that
its population is too large or too small as long as it can maintain the balance between the twin basic physical activities
of man—production and reproduction—between the existing
population and the resources available for its support. Generally speaking, the most desirable level of population is
also the one that attains the highest level of living, political
stability, and economic security, along with adequate freedom and leisure for the pursuit of creative and cultural
values.

Now arises the question of the relation between the size of
a country's population and the power exercised by it. It is

obvious that a nation of teeming millions is not necessarily a powerful nation, if the millions do not have the basic, irreducible, minimum needs of decent human existence like food, clothing, housing, education, and health services. India, with her 438,000,000, is not necessarily stronger than the United States of America or the Soviet Union, each with only about half of India's population. A country's total income may be taken as the single best index of its power. According to Dr. Cheng Chu-yuan, the per capita income of Communist China in 1952 was equivalent to about thirty-three U.S. dollars. In other words, the per capita income of the United States in 1952-1954 was forty-five times more than that of Communist China, and England's twenty times more. Thus from the national income point of view, China has not even caught up with India, whose per capita income in 1951-1952 was about fifty-eight U.S. dollars, not to speak of advanced Western nations. But this is only one consideration.

Secondly, the correlation between population and national power stems from the size of the labor force. While the statistics of the 1953 census may not be exact, they indicate that China has a very large and—in view of her age pyramid—youthful labor force.

The third factor is the availability of resources. During her long history, China has never undertaken a thorough geological survey of her entire land area. This omission is at present being remedied with the help of Soviet geological teams, and the reports now available indicate that the country has a great many natural resources awaiting development. And they are being developed at a faster rate than in any other Asian country.

The last consideration is the military aspect of the population problem. The creation of a sizable defense force—army, navy, and air services, and the ancillary personnel—depends upon the availability of people of a particular age group. A large army, for instance, is possible only where there is a

large population from which men of a particular age group
and in the necessary physical condition can be drawn. China
has this advantage.

All these considerations are relevant to any country. They
are particularly so in a totalitarian country with centralized
planning, complete control over the nation's material and
human resources, and known for its mass regimentation.
Such a country can create a formidable defense force. But
does this necessarily mean that a strong and unified China,
rapidly industrialized and mechanized and with a growing
fighting force, will be a source of aggression in the future?
This is a difficult question to answer, for much depends on
the scale of values and priorities that China will set before
herself.

Let us examine briefly the record of national situations—
both ideological and demographic—which have led to wars
in the past.

Germany, Italy, and Japan embarked upon a pro-natalist
policy and asked their people to multiply like rabbits. Birth
control and contraceptives were banned as so much decadent nonsense. A significant segment of the national income
was diverted to the production of arms and ammunition.
The increasing population was absorbed both in the new
factories that produced more guns, and in the growing
armies. And when the numbers grew beyond control, they
thought of building empires. The leaders began to argue
that they had a right to the good things of life beyond their
frontiers and belonging to other people. At the slightest pretext of wounded national honor or invaded rights, or with
no pretext at all, their armies began to march. And the world
was plunged into a holocaust. It is not necessary that a
nation should have real difficulties, economic or otherwise.
Even imagined grievances, if driven home strongly enough
—the people have no freedom to argue or protest—can spark
the tinder box and set off trouble.

A backward and impoverished China cannot start a war.

But it is a different matter with a united and strong China with a population spilling over her frontiers and with no emigration outlets. Even if China were a democracy with an abiding faith in freedom, her population numbers alone might cause concern in the minds of her neighbors. But unfortunately she has two strong factors which may conduce to her potential role as an aggressor. One is her Communist ideology—which attracts the faithful all over the world—and the other is the 11,000,000 overseas Chinese with their ethnic and cultural, if not political and ideological, solidarity with the mainland.

Communism has never been a purely *national* movement. The Comintern may have been abolished but the ideology is international in its appeal, strategy, and execution. Communists are missionaries *par excellence*. There is only one difference between religious missionaries and Communist political missionaries. The former attach some value to the means, but to the latter the end of proletarian revolution justifies any means. When the Communist leaders gained control in China, they first devoted themselves to putting their house in order and consolidating and stabilizing their power. But within a decade of their coming into power, they have launched an intellectual offensive to capture the youth of Asia. The battle for the minds of men, particularly the youth of Asia in the underdeveloped and uncommitted nations, has begun, as a visit to any bookshop in any large Asian city will testify.

There is a Communist Party in every Asian country, adopting tactics and maneuvers suited to the occasion and waiting to seize political power. All these Parties, no matter what their disclaimers and no matter how vociferously they affirm that they are purely *national* movements, look up to Mother Russia (and Father Khrushchev) and Sister China (and Brother Mao) for ideological inspiration and moral support.

The tactics of the Communist Parties in Asia range from plain arson, banditry, and murder as in Malaya, armed revolt and different degrees of civil war as in Burma, Indochina, and Indonesia, to the battle of the ballot box in India, Ceylon, and Pakistan. And in India the Communists gained a respectable, democratic foothold for a short time in the state of Kerala. A foreign diplomat asked the then Chief Minister Namboodiripad what spectacular things he had accomplished since the Communists' coming into power in Kerala. "We cannot do very much, for India's Constitution comes in the way," he is reported to have replied. But he went on to add, "If you know you are going to be born a dog in your next life, you don't start barking now." The Indian Constitution may be an obstacle to a dictatorship of the proletariat in Kerala, but "constitutional Communism"—a contradiction in terms—has already begun in Asia, and who can tell what will be the future?

Judging from the interest evinced in Kerala by my Communist friends in China, I know they are watching this unique way to "democratic dictatorship" with great interest. And given their idealism—and Communists are idealistic—their messianic fervor, their missionary zeal, their opportunistic tactics, and their methods with no holds barred, Communism is bound to make headway unless the peoples of Asia and the world are given a real stake in freedom and democracy through ever-rising levels of living which assure the dignity and worth of human beings.

In 1949, Liu Shao-chi, writing on "Internationalism and Nationalism," pointed out: "The Communists in such other colonial and semi-colonial countries as India, Burma, Assam, the Philippines, Indonesia, Indochina, and South Korea must for the sake of their national interests similarly adopt a firm and irreconcilable policy against national betrayal by the reactionary section of the *bourgeoisie,* especially the big *bourgeoisie,* which has already surrendered to imperialism. If this were not done, it would be a grave mistake."

The second source of help to the spread of Chinese Communism and its intellectual hegemony in South Asia will be the 14,000,000 overseas Chinese. Every country, with the exception of India, has a sizable Chinese minority constituting a potential threat to the political freedom and the various national ways of life in the lands of this region. Out of Thailand's 20,000,000 people, the Chinese number more than 3,000,000. In Singapore, nearly 80 per cent of a total of 1,000,000 people are Chinese. In Malaya proper, the Chinese number more than 1,500,000. Indonesia has about 2,000,000 Chinese, Laos and Cambodia about 500,000, and Burma some 20,000. Only in India do the Chinese constitute a microscopic minority.

Peking runs a Department of Overseas Chinese Affairs. China, through the centuries, has claimed all Chinese as her citizens, no matter where they are born or where they make a living. How else can one explain the Chinese *national* census presenting the nation's total population figures inclusive of the overseas Chinese who are nationals of other countries?

In the last few years, China has begun to build "Overseas Chinese Villages"—neat, modern suburban communities near big cities like Canton and Peking. I visited the one near Canton. Modern colonies with all the latest amenities and conveniences, having their own schools and social services, have been built to attract the overseas Chinese. I learned that Communist China was anxious to attract the savings of the overseas Chinese who would like to return to their homeland, invest their savings in the People's Republic, retire and die in New China. But since these people, accustomed to comfort and a free way of life, might not return to China to barter their precious savings for a regimented way of life, the Overseas Villages have been made very different from the rest of China—apparently as a temporary expedient until the government has collected enough of their savings to make this unusual treatment no longer worthwhile. There are cars and refrigerators, books and washing machines, and the life they can live in them is not dissimilar to the life that they led abroad, though it is certainly very different from that led by the rest of China's population. I met Chinese who had been successful businessmen and traders in such countries as Brazil and Panama, Indonesia and Malaya. They said that they had repatriated their savings and had invested them in the various "joint enterprises" (government- and privately-owned working together) and had retired to lead a life of ease.

The reason for these Overseas Chinese Villages is not only to attract the much-needed exchange provided by the savings of the former residents abroad, but to use their good offices to indoctrinate the many whom they have left behind.

Will China ever claim the territories where her children have settled and become large minorities? She has made no official claims except to Tibet (and here successfully), Taiwan, Hong Kong, and Macao. Kowloon and the Leased Territory can revert to the mainland when the lease to the British expires.

But Mao Tse-tung, writing some twenty years ago, pointed out: "In defeating China in war, the imperialist powers have taken away many Chinese dependent states and a part of her territories. Japan took Korea, Taiwan, and the Ryukyu Islands, the Pescadores, Port Arthur; England seized Burma, Bhutan, and Hong Kong; France occupied Annam, and even an insignificant country like Portugal took Macao." Does China now claim all these territories? No, not yet.

But in the face of all this, it may be foolish to assume that the Chinese Communists will go back to their Middle Kingdom and ignore the "barbarians beyond their gates."

II

8

Tibet

On March 21, 1959, a news report from New Delhi's All-India Radio informed the world that fighting had broken out in Lhasa, Tibet's capital, between the Tibetans, who wanted to preserve their own free way of life, and the Chinese Communists, who wanted to impose Communism on Tibet.

For some weeks informed people in India and other countries bordering on China knew that serious trouble had been smoldering in Tibet. The Tibetans had been resisting the large influx of Chinese Communist cadres and troops with their countless demands on the Tibetan people.

About the beginning of March, relations between the Chinese Communists and the Tibetans became strained when the Dalai Lama, Tibet's spiritual and temporal leader, was "invited" to proceed to Peking. When he failed to obey, he was ordered to present himself to the Chinese authorities in Lhasa without his usual, traditional bodyguard of some hundred men. This order, though ignored by the Dalai Lama, was sufficient to arouse strong resentment among the Tibetans. They showed their hostility by holding anti-Chinese demonstrations and by voicing their determination to prevent the Dalai Lama from leaving his palace and to thwart any Communist attempt to arrest him.

Tibetan officials claimed that the reason for the Dalai Lama's failure to proceed to Peking in answer to the summons from the Chinese capital was that he had to perform his traditional duty of touring the country's monasteries during that time of the year and consequently it was impossible for him to make this trip.

But the real reason behind the Dalai Lama's refusal to go

to Peking was a very different one. The officials close to the Dalai Lama were apprehensive that, once he reached Peking, he would be put under the "protection" of the Communist authorities, never to return to Lhasa. This fear was not without some basis, for the mere presence of the Dalai Lama in the Potala palace lent a kind of moral support to the silent resistance of the Tibetans to the inroads the Chinese Communists were making into the Forbidden Land. And the Chinese realized that the Dalai Lama's tour of monasteries would only strengthen Tibetan resistance to the Communist regime. The Chinese had ordered a plane to stand by ready to fly the Dalai Lama to Peking at a moment's notice. They had hoped that with the Dalai Lama out of Lhasa and safely installed as their "guest" in Peking, they would have a better chance of winning the Tibetans to Communism.

The immediate reason that precipitated the Tibetan revolt, however, was this: the Dalai Lama had accepted an invitation by the Chinese General stationed in Lhasa to witness a cultural show, but when the date for the performance was suddenly moved ahead, the Tibetans became apprehensive that the Dalai Lama's invitation to it might have some sinister purpose, and fighting broke out.

The Tibetan General who led the revolt had some 25,000 devoted Khamba tribesmen at his command, and these were joined by outraged, patriotic Tibetans from Lhasa and other areas in Tibet. The plan of the rebellious group was not made clear. However, they launched an all-out offensive to drive out the Chinese Communist Liberation Army stationed near Lhasa.

But it was an unequal fight from the very beginning. The revolt, a spontaneous uprising, was apparently not well planned. The poorly-equipped Tibetans stood no chance against the well-equipped, superior Chinese forces. The Tibetans were simply mowed down. Some 13,000 monks are reported to have joined the Khamba tribesmen, and the number of Tibetan rebels became large, but they proved a poor match against the Communist forces, which used artillery and automatic weapons.

By March 25, the Tibetan fight for freedom had been more or less put down by the Chinese, who had moved a large body of troops with machine guns and other modern weapons into Lhasa. But sporadic fighting went on for several days in different parts of Tibet. The only disadvantage the Communist troops suffered was unfamiliarity with the difficult mountain terrain. The Tibetans cut communications and resorted to guerrilla fighting. This, of course, aided the resistance, but not for long.

The Supreme Tibetan Council, calling upon its countrymen to continue the battle, denounced the Chinese occupation of Tibet, declared Tibet's independence of Peking, and demanded that the Communist occupation forces be immediately withdrawn. The Council assured the Tibetan people that the question of Tibet would be brought before the United Nations. The last that the outside world heard from the Council was that they would fight for Tibet's freedom to the last man. "As long as there is a single Tibetan alive, we will fight our Chinese oppressors. And God will punish the Chinese Communists."

While India and the world watched this unequal fight helplessly, the Peking regime itself remained silent for a whole week, neither confirming nor contradicting the Tibetan struggle for freedom. But on March 28, Peking broadcast an order of the State Council of the People's Republic of China, signed by Mr. Chou En-lai, the Prime Minister. It said in part:

> Most of the *kaloons** of the Tibetan local government
> and the reactionary clique of the upper social strata
> colluded with imperialism, gathered together rebellious

---

* The local government of Tibet is called *kasha*, and its six members are called *kaloons* in Tibetan.

bandits, rebelled, wrought havoc among the people,
held the Dalai Lama under duress, tore up the seven-
teen-article "Agreement on Measures for the Peaceful
Liberation of Tibet" and, on the night of March 19,
directed the Tibetan local army and rebels in an all-out
attack against the People's Liberation Army garrison
in Lhasa. Such acts, which betray the motherland and
disrupt the unification of the country, cannot be tolerated by the law.

To safeguard the unification of the country and national
unity, in addition to enjoining the Tibet Military Area
Command of the Chinese People's Liberation Army to
put down the rebellion thoroughly, it has been decided
that, as from today, the Tibetan local government is dissolved and that its functions and powers will be exercised by the Preparatory Committee for the Tibet
Autonomous Region. During the time when the Dalai
Lama, Chairman of the Preparatory Committee for the
Tibet Autonomous Region, is held under duress, Panchen Lama, Vice-Chairman of the Preparatory Committee, shall act as Chairman of the said Preparatory
Committee. . . .

Eighteen traitors [whose names are given] are hereby
dismissed from their posts as members of the Preparatory Committee for the Tibet Autonomous Region and
from all their other posts and shall be punished respectively according to law. . . .

. . . The [new] Preparatory Committee for the Tibet
Autonomous Region will lead all the people of Tibet,
ecclesiastical and secular, to unite as one and make
common efforts to assist the People's Liberation Army
in putting down the rebellion quickly, to strengthen
the national defense, protect the interests of the people
of all nationalities, maintain social order, and strive for
the building of a democratic and socialist new Tibet.

II

When the news of the Tibetan revolt leaked out, both Peking and the free world began to wonder about the whereabouts of the Dalai Lama. At first, the Dalai Lama was reported to be under arrest in his Potala palace in Lhasa. But a few days later, according to some reports, he, along with the members of his cabinet, was supposed to be leading the rebels from an unknown hideout beyond the reach of the Chinese occupation forces. A few days later, it became obvious that the Peking authorities were making a desperate search for the Dalai Lama. They asked the governments concerned for permission to search the Indian, Nepalese, and Bhutan diplomatic missions in Lhasa for him, but when they were informed that the Dalai Lama was not in any of the missions, they did not press the request.

However, when the Peking regime realized that their search for the Dalai Lama had been in vain, they issued a State Council order, as already observed, to the effect that the Dalai Lama was being held under duress by the rebels. The Tibetan Supreme Council was dissolved. Pending the Dalai Lama's return to the throne, the Panchen Lama was proclaimed the new Chairman of the Preparatory Committee for the Tibet Autonomous Region.

The Panchen Lama, who is regarded by many as a mere puppet since he is a protégé of the Chinese Communists, promptly accepted the appointment and promised full support to the Chinese occupation forces in putting down the revolt and thoroughly smashing "the shameless, traitorous intrigues carried out by the upper-strata reactionary clique with the aid of the imperialists and the Chiang Kai-shek clique."

While the fighting between the Tibetan Khamba rebels and the Communist troops had been going on, the Dalai Lama, accompanied by his mother, sister, and brother, members of his cabinet, and an entourage of about a hundred people, left the palace and made his way out of Tibet. The caravan's steep and rugged route, kept a top secret, was guarded by advance cavalrymen and Khamba tribesmen who alone knew the craggy and precipitous path leading out of Tibet. They were aware that the Chinese troops were searching for them and that Communist paratroopers had been dropped at various passes to prevent their escape. The party traveled by night, hiding by day in lamaseries, hamlets, and Khamba encampments which had been secretly alerted by scouting forerunners that the entourage was on its way. After an arduous journey of fourteen days and nights along the 15,000-foot-high mountainous terrain, the Dalai Lama and his party, having successfully eluded the Communist searchers, reached Towang, a little village on the Indian side of the frontier. The Dalai Lama asked for, and was granted, political asylum in India.

A few days later, the Dalai Lama reached Tezpur and issued a statement to the press which clarified the issues behind the Tibetan revolt. His statement made it clear that there had been no truth in the Communist allegations that he was "under duress" and "a captive of the rebels" or that the revolt had been engineered by imperialist agents from the Indian frontier town of Kalimpong.

The following text of the Dalai Lama's first statement to the press at Tezpur on April 18, 1959, is reproduced here in full, for this statement released a flood of Chinese protests and accusations against India:

It had always been accepted that the Tibetan people are different from the Han people of China. There has always been a strong desire for independence on the part of the Tibetan people. Throughout history, this has been asserted on numerous occasions. Sometimes the Chinese government has imposed its suzerainty on Tibet, and at other times Tibet has functioned as an independent country.

In any event, at all times, even when the suzerainty of China was imposed, Tibet remained autonomous, in control of its internal affairs.

In 1951, under pressure of the Chinese government, a seventeen-point agreement was made between China and Tibet. In that agreement the suzerainty of China was accepted as there was no alternative left to the Tibetans. But even in the agreement, it was stated that Tibet would enjoy full autonomy. Though the control of external events was to be in the hands of the Chinese government, it was agreed that there would be no interference by the Chinese government with the Tibetan religion and customs and her internal administration. In fact, after the occupation of Tibet by the Chinese armies, the Tibetan government did not enjoy any measure of autonomy even in internal matters, and the Chinese government exercised full powers in Tibetan affairs.

In 1956, a Preparatory Committee was set up for Tibet, with the Dalai Lama as Chairman and the Panchen Lama as Vice-Chairman and General Chang Kuo Hua as the representative of the Chinese government. In practice, even this body had little power, and decisions in all important matters were made by the Chinese authorities. The Dalai Lama and his government tried their best to adhere to the seventeen-point agreement, but the interference of the Chinese authorities persisted. By the end of 1955, a struggle had started in the Khan Province, and this assumed serious proportions in 1956. In the consequential struggle, the Chinese armed forces destroyed a large number of monasteries.

Many lamas were killed, and a large number of monks and officials were taken and employed on the construction of roads in China, and the interference in the exercise of religious freedom increased.

The relations of the Tibetans with China became openly strained from the early part of February, 1959. The Dalai Lama had agreed a month in advance to attend a cultural show in the Chinese headquarters, and the date was suddenly fixed for March 10. The people of Lhasa became apprehensive that some harm might be done to the Dalai Lama and, as a result, some 10,000 people gathered around the Dalai Lama's summer palace at Norbulingka and physically prevented the Dalai Lama from attending the function.

Thereafter, the people themselves decided to raise a bodyguard for the protection of the Dalai Lama. Large crowds of Tibetans went about the streets of Lhasa, demonstrating against the Chinese rule in Tibet. Two days later, thousands of Tibetan women held demonstrations protesting against Chinese authority. In spite of this demonstration from the people, the Dalai Lama and his government endeavored to maintain friendly relations with the Chinese and tried to carry out negotiations with the Chinese representatives as to how best to bring about peace in Tibet and assuage the people's anxiety.

While these negotiations were being carried out, reinforcements arrived to strengthen the Chinese garrisons in Lhasa and Tibet. On March 17, two or three mortar shells were fired in the direction of the Norbulingka Palace. Fortunately the shells fell in a nearby pond.

After this, the advisers became alive to the danger to the person of the Dalai Lama, and in those difficult circumstances it became imperative for the Dalai Lama, the members of his family, and his high officials to leave Lhasa.

The Dalai Lama would like to state categorically that he left Lhasa and Tibet and came to India of his own free will and not under duress.

It was due to the loyalty and affectionate support of his people that the Dalai Lama was able to find his way through a route which was quite arduous. The route which the Dalai Lama took involved the crossing of the Kyichu and Tsangpo rivers, making his way through the Lhoka area, Yarlung valley, and Psonadgong before reaching the Indian frontier at Kanzeymane near Chuttanmu.

On March 29, 1959, the Dalai Lama sent emissaries to cross the Indo-Tibetan border, requesting the Indian government's permission to enter India and seek asylum there. The Dalai Lama is extremely grateful to the people and the government of India for their spontaneous and generous welcome as well as for the asylum granted to him and his followers.

India and Tibet have had religious, cultural, and trade links for over a thousand years, and for Tibet, India has always been the land of enlightenment, having given birth to the Lord Buddha. The Dalai Lama is deeply touched by the kind greetings extended to him on his safe arrival in India by the Prime Minister, Mr. Jawaharlal Nehru, and his colleagues in the government of India.

Ever since the Dalai Lama entered at Kanzeymane, near Chuttanmu, he has experienced in a full measure the respect and hospitality extended to him by the people of the Kameng Frontier Division of the Northeast Frontier Agency, and the Dalai Lama would like to state how the government of India's officers posted there had spared no effort in making his stay and journey through this extremely well-administered part of India as comfortable as possible.

The Dalai Lama will now be proceeding to Mussoorie, which he hopes to reach in the next few days. The Dalai Lama will give thought to his future plans, and, if necessary, give expression to them as soon as he has had a chance to rest and reflect on recent events.

His country and people have passed through an extremely difficult period, and all that the Dalai Lama wishes to say at the moment is to express his sincere regret at the tragedy which has overtaken Tibet and to hope fervently that these troubles will be over soon, without any more bloodshed.

As the Dalai Lama and the spiritual head of all the Buddhists in Tibet, his foremost concern is the well-being of his people and ensuring the perpetual flourishing of his sacred religion and the freedom of his country.

While expressing once again thankfulness at his safe arrival in India, the Dalai Lama would like to take this opportunity to communicate to all his friends, well-wishers, and devotees in India and abroad his sincere gratitude for the many messages of sympathy and concern with which they have flooded him.

This statement of the Dalai Lama gave the lie to the Chinese assertions that the Tibetan revolt was engineered by foreign, imperialist agents and "upper-strata reactionary" Tibetans, that it was directed from the Indian frontier town of Kalimpong, and that the Dalai Lama was being held "under duress."

The discomfiture of the Chinese Communists, smarting under the defeat of having let the Dalai Lama slip through their fingers, was not improved by his Tezpur statement. They immediately started a barrage of anti-Indian propaganda. They screamed that the Dalai Lama's statement was a forgery and that the author of the statement could well be an official of the Ministry of External Affairs of the government of India! India had become expansionist and was casting covetous eyes on Tibet. Prime Minister Nehru was accused of deviation and siding with China's enemies. The entire Chinese nation was made to take up the new anti-Indian slogans.

And just as well perhaps, for unsuspecting India realized, as she never had before, the kind of China she had been championing for the last decade. The mask was dropped. The true face of Communism in all its naked terror was revealed.

The Tibetan revolt for freedom focused the free world's attention on this isolated, little-known mountain plateau and its people. The rebellion not only demonstrated to uncommitted Asia the nature of the Peking regime and the shape of things to come by way of the new Red colonialism, but brought to light the uneasy relations between India and China. India is Communist China's great friend, but only as long as the friend does everything to please and nothing to irritate China. To a lot of Indian politicians, the Tibetan revolt revealed in a month what nearly ten years of Chinese Communism had not—the nature of the regime with which India has been coexisting.

III

The plateau of Tibet, the veritable "roof of the world," covering an area of about 463,000 square miles, stretches from Kashmir on the west to the Chinese provinces of Chinghai and the Sinkiang Uighur Autonomous Region, and on the south to the three Himalayan kingdoms of Nepal, Bhutan, and Sikkim, and to the plateau of Upper Assam, India's Northeastern Frontier Province.

Tibet's population is less than 3,000,000 and, by virtue of her theocratic social structure, monks constitute a third of the adult male population. The rural population is composed of sheep and cattle-raising nomads as well as settled agriculturists in the valleys, where barley, rice, wheat, tea, and mustard are grown. The people in the three cities of

Tibet are engaged in entrepôt trade on the caravan routes to India, Bhutan, Sikkim, and China. They export hides, skins, and wool and import a wide variety of manufactured goods, mainly from India.

Southern Tibet is densely populated, for here in the valleys, at the relatively low altitude of 12,000 feet, are the flat plains that render cultivation and grazing possible. Here also are located Tibet's three cities of Lhasa, Shigatse, and Gyangtse. The city of Lhasa, with its 70,000 people, is the political and spiritual capital of Tibet and is her commercial and economic center as well. Lhasa is lorded over by the incredibly magnificent Potala palace, the winter residence of the Dalai Lama and the Vatican of Lamaism. Potala was built in the seventeenth century by the fifth Dalai Lama, and it was this Dalai Lama who also created the office of Panchen Lama to honor his favorite teacher, giving him a new name, Panchen ("Teacher") Lama, and assigning to his keeping Tibet's second largest city, Shigatse, and its monasteries.

IV

Tibet's known history dates from only the seventh century when Buddhism arrived from India, though legendary accounts of the country's earlier annals are not wanting. From all the available records, Tibet had been an independent country for centuries, and not a part of the Middle Kingdom as believed by some.

As early as 635 A.D., Tibet was ruled by a famous Tibetan king, Sengtson Gompo. There were, of course, contacts between Lhasa and China, but they were such as exist between independent nations with diplomatic exchanges. In fact, in 641 A.D., the Tibetan king married Princess Wen Cheng, the daughter of the Chinese ruler Tai Tsung of the Tang dynasty. During the reign of Tihtsong Detsen, about 741

A.D., China paid a yearly tribute of some 50,000 yards of Chinese brocade to Tibet.

It was in 1244 that Lamaism, more or less as we know it today, was introduced, and it was then that the first Lama king ruled over Tibet. It is true that the Mongols and Manchus, alien dynasties to China, attempted to conquer and establish their rule over Tibet, and with some success; but this imposition of alien power did not last very long. For these alien dynasties were busy conquering a better prize— China herself. At the end of the eighteenth century, the Manchus tried to impose their rule on Tibet, but the country was never successfully integrated with the Chinese Empire.

In 1910, the Manchus, on the eve of their downfall, invaded Tibet, and the Dalai Lama fled to Darjeeling. He was deposed by an imperial decree of the Old Buddha (as the Empress Dowager was called), but the Manchu Dynasty itself was overthrown by the Chinese Nationalist Revolution in 1911. The Dalai Lama returned to Lhasa in 1912 and drove out the Chinese garrison stationed there.

The government of the Chinese Republic, despite their preoccupation with maintaining their all but absent political stability at home, dispatched a punitive expedition to Tibet to assert China's suzerain, not sovereign, power. But this expedition came to nothing, for the British in India intervened on the ground that such action on the part of Peking constituted a violation of the Anglo-Chinese Treaty of 1906. The British did not dispute China's suzerainty over Tibet but could not concede China's assertion of sovereignty since Tibet had independent treaty relations with the British government. Further, the fact that China and Tibet exchanged diplomatic and other missions periodically proved Tibet's independent status.

However, the British invited the Chinese government to negotiate a tripartite agreement that would clearly define the political status as well as the geographical frontiers of

Tibet. Replying to this, the Chinese government declared that they had no intention of reducing Tibet to the level of a Chinese province, that they would scrupulously respect both the integrity and the traditional system of Tibetan government, and hence saw no reason for a new treaty. In the meanwhile the Tibetans drove the last of the Chinese forces out of Lhasa. And on January 11, 1913, the Dalai Lama concluded a treaty with the sovereign republic of Outer Mongolia, as between two free countries, and thus proclaimed Tibet's independence.

The British government pursued the matter further and renewed their proposal for a tripartite conference, which was ultimately accepted by both China and Tibet. The conference was held at Simla on October 13, 1913. Great Britain was represented by Sir A. H. McMahon, China by Mr. Ivan Chen, and Tibet by her Prime Minister, Mr. Long Chen Shatra.

This tripartite Simla conference evolved the "Simla Convention," by which China's nominal suzerainty over Tibet and its right to maintain a mission in Lhasa were recognized, but China was forbidden to interfere in any way with Tibetan internal administration. The convention also differentiated between the complete autonomy of the Inner Zone and the semi-autonomy of the Outer Zone of Tibet. The agreement was initialed by all the three representatives, but the action of the Chinese representative was disavowed by the Chinese government, which declined to ratify the treaty, not because they objected to any specific provision of the Convention but because of their unwillingness to accept the geographical definitions of the frontiers of Outer Tibet as proposed in the Convention. Thus nothing came of the Simla Convention.

The British continued to maintain that Tibet was autonomous, though China had suzerainty over Tibet. China, on the other hand, continued to assert that Tibet was theoretically an integral part of China. Tibet, of course, considered herself independent of China and, for that matter, of any other country.

The McMahon Line, named after Sir A. H. McMahon, the British representative at the Simla tripartite conference of 1913, delineates the frontier between India and Tibet. The frontier follows for about 850 miles eastward from Bhutan along the spur of the Himalayas and the northern and north-eastern borders of Assam to the point of intersection of the Burmese, Chinese, and Tibetan frontiers. At a point, near the ninety-fifth meridian, the frontier is broken by the Brahmaputra river.

The McMahon Line, thus defined, was incorporated in the Simla Convention, but, as already pointed out, the Convention was not ratified by the Chinese government.

In the next few years, when China was fully engrossed with her own internal political troubles and when the edicts of the Peking government did not go beyond the gates of a few cities, the Chinese general in charge of the garrison on the Sino-Tibetan border, without any provocation, started hostilities against Tibet, only to encounter the Tibetan army's determined resistance. They not only resisted but defeated the Chinese, recapturing certain frontier Tibetan areas that China had annexed earlier. The Chinese there-upon had to seek the good offices of the British consular agent in Tibet to mediate and restore peace. The Chinese learned at some cost, but unfortunately not for long, that the Tibetans, like any people anywhere, do not like to be pushed around.

In 1930 both Britain and China established quasi-diplomatic missions in Lhasa. And during World War II, Tibet not only opened her own department of foreign affairs but "asserted her complete independence" by remaining neutral and not throwing her forces on the side of China.

During the British rule in India, relations between India and Tibet were cordial and were carried out from 1930 through an Agent of the Indian Political Department stationed in Lhasa. In 1947, when she regained her political freedom, India inherited from Britain, on the basis of treaty rights between Tibet and the British government in India, the rights to: 1.) station an Indian political agent in Lhasa; 2.) maintain trade agencies at Gyangtse, Gartok, and Yatung; 3.) run the postal and telegraph offices along the trade route up to Gyangtse; and 4.) station a small military escort for the protection of this commercial highway. In 1947 the government of India appointed an Indian officer as the head of the Indian Mission in Lhasa.

But while the Chinese government continued to claim some strange, non-existent sovereignty over Tibet, it could not exercise even nominal suzerainty from the time of the downfall of the Manchu Dynasty in 1910 and the Nationalist Revolution in 1911 to the defeat of the Kuomintang government and the accession of the Communists to power in 1949.

In fact, in 1950, when the Communists began to cast their covetous eyes on Tibet, she contended in her appeal to the United Nations that China by her refusal to ratify the Simla Convention had renounced "the benefits that would have accrued to her" under the Convention, and consequently Tibet was politically independent, *de jure*.

V

But the Dalai Lama and the Tibetan government knew only too well that, whenever a government in China became stable and had energy and strength to spare, its first urge was to expand and conquer Tibet. When the Communists became entrenched in power and began to consolidate their political gains in 1950, Tibet knew that before long she would receive their unwelcome attention.

In November, 1949, Prime Minister Nehru told a press conference in London that India's relations with Tibet were always conducted on the assumption that she was an autonomous country, though China's nominal suzerainty over Tibet was recognized. On December 29, 1949, India recognized the Chinese Communist regime in Peking. On January 1, 1950, the Peking government proclaimed that one of the "basic tasks" of the People's Liberation Army was "the liberation of Tibet."

Disturbed over her prospective "liberation" by Peking, the Tibetan government organized missions to India, the United States, Britain, and Nepal to canvas support for Tibet's territorial integrity. Peking labeled these proposed missions "illegal" and contended that their reception by any country was "an unfriendly and hostile act."

These missions, however, did not materialize, and, instead, a Tibetan mission was persuaded to come to Peking, obviously to negotiate "Tibet's liberation." But nothing really came of this delegation to Peking either, for the Communists had their own private plans for Tibet.

In April, 1950, a Tibetan mission composed of seven prominent dignitaries appointed by the Dalai Lama's government in Lhasa arrived in India to contact China's representative in New Delhi to explore avenues of better Sino-Tibetan relations and amicably settle the differences between the two countries. The mission explained that the Dalai Lama preferred his delegation to meet Chinese representatives in a neutral country like India rather than in China itself, for understandable reasons.

This mission, with its headquarters in Kalimpong, made preliminary contacts in New Delhi, and as the Chinese ambassador had not yet arrived in India, decided to proceed to Hong Kong to meet representatives of the Peking government there. The British authorities in Hong Kong, however, refused visas for the delegation on the grounds that it would complicate the then "delicate situation," that its diplomatic status was doubtful, and that both India and Britain had recognized the Peking regime. Thereupon, the Tibetan mission stayed on in India until the Chinese ambassador arrived in New Delhi in September. Negotiations between him and the Tibetan mission took place, but they ended with nothing more than a promise by the Chinese ambassador that the conversations would be reported to Peking.

The government of India suggested that the Tibetan mission should proceed to Peking and negotiate directly with the Peking government. But while arrangements were being made for the Tibetan mission to go to Peking, news arrived that Peking had dispatched Chinese troops to "liberate Tibet"! With the news of this invasion of Tibet by China, the Tibetan mission's projected visit to Peking was naturally cancelled.

On October 24, 1950, the New China News Agency announced that Peking had ordered the Chinese troops to advance into Tibet "to liberate 3,000,000 Tibetans from imperialist aggression, to complete the unification of China, and to safeguard the frontier regions of the country."

On October 26, 1950, the government of India, according to an announcement of the Ministry of External Affairs, sent a note to the Chinese government expressing "surprise and regret" at the invasion in the midst of negotiations between Lhasa and Peking and "deploring" the fact that China should have sought a solution of her problems with that country "by force instead of by the slower and more enduring methods of peaceful approach."

In their reply to this note, dated October 30, 1950, the Chinese asserted that Tibet was "an integral part of Chinese territory" and that the matter "is entirely a domestic problem of China, and no foreign interference will be tolerated." The reply stated further: "The Chinese People's Liberation Army must enter Tibet, liberate the Tibetan people, and defend the frontiers of China. . . . With regard to the viewpoint of the government of India on what it regards as deplorable, the Central People's Government cannot but consider it as having been affected by foreign influences hostile to China in Tibet."

On October 31, 1950, the government of India sent a second

note of protest to Peking "categorically repudiating" the charge in the Chinese reply that the Indian government's stand was affected by anti-Chinese foreign influences. The note pointed out: "It is with no desire to interfere that the government of India has sought earnestly that the settlement of the Tibetan problem should be effected by peaceful negotiations, adjusting the legitimate Tibetan claim to autonomy within the framework of Chinese suzerainty. . . . Tibetan autonomy is a fact which the Chinese government was itself willing to recognize."

The Chinese government's reply to this second protest reiterated the new view that "China possessed sovereign rights in Tibet" and strangely enough accused India of "blocking a peaceful settlement" in Tibet in order to "prevent the Chinese government from exercising its sovereign rights in that country."

On December 6, 1950, Prime Minister Nehru pointed out in the Indian Parliament that, while India wanted the Tibetan question to be settled peacefully, China continued to talk of the "liberation of Tibet," and he confessed that it was not clear "from *whom* the Chinese were going to liberate Tibet." Presumably the Tibetans!

"The Chinese invasion of Tibet," as a recent pamphlet on Tibet puts it, "perturbed the Prime Minister for other reasons also. On October 8, 1950, the U.N. forces in Korea crossed the thirty-eighth parallel, and New Delhi was trying its best to prevent this conflict from spreading and was consistently championing China's admission to the U.N. India had put and professed her faith in the peaceful intention of China and had been assured by the Chinese Communist government that the latter would solve the Tibetan problem by peaceful means. But India was tragically betrayed by the Communist rulers of China. This invasion, therefore, came as a rude shock to India, and it shattered once and for all the tranquillity of India's northern frontiers."

When the actual Chinese invasion of Tibet began, the

Dalai Lama requested the government of India to bring up the issue of Chinese aggression before the United Nations. It was announced at that time that India would support Tibet's case to the extent of censuring China for using force against Tibet. On November 7, 1950, Tibet submitted her complaint to the United Nations. It ran in part as follows:

> It is in the belief that aggression will not go unchecked in any part of the world that we have assumed the responsibility of reporting the recent happenings in the border area of Tibet to the United Nations. The problem of Tibet has taken on alarming proportions in recent times. This problem is not of Tibet's making but is largely the outcome of unthwarted Chinese ambitions to bring weaker nations on her periphery within her active domination.
>
> There were times when Tibet sought, but seldom received, the protection of the Chinese Empire. The Chinese, however, in their natural urge for expansion, have wholly misconstrued the significance of the time of friendship and interdependence that existed between China and Tibet as between neighbors. To them China was a suzerain and Tibet a vassal state. It is this which first aroused legitimate apprehension in the mind of Tibet regarding the designs of China on her independent status. Chinese conduct during their expeditions in 1910 completed the rupture between the two countries in 1911-1912, when Tibet, under the thirteenth Dalai Lama, declared her complete independence, even as Nepal simultaneously broke away from allegiance to China. The Chinese Revolution of 1911 . . . snapped the last sentimental and religious bonds between Tibet and China. Tibet thereafter depended entirely on her isolation, her faith in the wisdom of the Lord Buddha,

and occasionally on support of the British in India for protection.

In 1914 British persuasion led Tibet to sign a treaty which superimposed on her the nominal suzerainty of China, and by which the Chinese were accorded the right to maintain a mission in Lhasa, though they were strictly forbidden to interfere in the internal affairs of Tibet. Apart from the fact, even the nominal suzerainty which Tibet conceded to China is not enforceable because of the non-signing of the treaty of 1914 by the Chinese. Tibet maintained independent relations with other neighboring countries such as India and Nepal. Furthermore she did not compromise her position by throwing in her forces in World War II on the side of China. Thus she asserted and maintained her complete independence.

The treaty of 1914 still guides relations between Tibet and India, and the Chinese, not being a party to it, may be taken to have renounced the benefits that would have otherwise accrued to them from the treaty. Tibet's independence thereby reassumed *de jure* status. . . . The slender tie that Tibet maintained with China after the 1911 Revolution became less justifiable when China underwent a further revolution and turned into a full-fledged Communist state. . . . Foreseeing future complications, the Tibetan government broke off diplomatic relations with China and made the Chinese representative in Lhasa depart from Tibet in July, 1949. Since then Tibet has not even maintained formal relations with the Chinese government. She desires to live apart, uncontaminated by the germ of a highly materialistic creed.

. . . This unwarranted act of aggression has not only disturbed the peace of Tibet but is in complete disregard of a solemn assurance given by the Chinese to the government of India. It has created a grave situation and may eventually deprive Tibet of her long-cherished independence.

Tibet will not go down without a fight, though there is little hope of a nation dedicated to peace resisting the brutal efforts of men trained to war. But we understand that the United Nations has decided to stop aggression wherever it takes place. The armed invasion for the incorporation of Tibet within the folds of Chinese Communism through sheer physical force is a clear case of aggression. As long as the people of Tibet are compelled by force to become a part of China against their will and consent, the invasion of Tibet will be the grossest instance of the violation of the weak by the strong.

We therefore appeal to the nations of the world to intercede on our behalf and restrain Chinese aggression. The problem is simple. The Chinese claim Tibet as part of China. Tibetans feel that racially, culturally, and geographically they are apart from the Chinese. . . . The conquest of Tibet by China will only enlarge the area of conflict and increase the threat to the independence of other Asian countries. With the approval of His Holiness the Dalai Lama, we entrust the problem of Tibet in this emergency to the ultimate decision of the United Nations, in the hope that the conscience of the world will not allow the disruption of our state by methods reminiscent of the jungle.

(Signed by the members of the Tibetan cabinet [*Kashag*] and the Tibetan National Assembly [*Tsongdu*].)

When this appeal was submitted to the United Nations, the Salvadorean delegate to the U.N. called on the United Nations, on November 18, to condemn Communist China for her "unprovoked aggression" against Tibet and proposed the creation of a special committee to study the measures that could be taken by the U.N. General Assembly to assist Tibet. But when the proposal came before the Assembly's Steering Committee, India unfortunately reversed her stand and suggested that the Tibetan complaint should be dropped. As no one else was prepared to sponsor Tibet's complaint of China's aggression, it was shelved indefinitely.

The Communist troops penetrated into Tibet as far as the borders of the Tibetan capital and halted there. In March, 1951, the Tibetan government sent a new mission to Peking to negotiate with the Chinese government the future of Tibet. These negotiations resulted in a seventeen-point Sino-Tibetan Agreement on March 23, 1951, annexing Tibet into the Republic of China. This Agreement was characterized by the Dalai Lama later, when he escaped from Lhasa and obtained political asylum in India in April, 1959, as an agreement signed by the Tibetans "under compulsion."

This Sino-Tibetan Agreement provided:

1.) That Tibet would enjoy regional autonomy and the Chinese Central Government would not interfere with its political institutions and internal administration.

2.) That the Chinese Central Government would be responsible for Tibet's foreign relations.

3.) That the Chinese army would enter Tibet to "strengthen national defense" and would gradually reorganize and absorb the Tibetan armed forces.

4.) That the Chinese Central Government would recognize and maintain the Dalai Lama's position; that the Panchen Lama would be allowed to return to the part of Tibet formerly ruled by his predecessors, and that religious freedom would be protected.

5.) That the Tibetan Regional Government would voluntarily carry out reforms without interference from the Chinese Central Government and that the latter would assist the Tibetan people in their political, economic, industrial, commercial, cultural, and educational development.

6.) That Tibetan officials and others who had collaborated with "imperialism" and the Kuomintang would not be prosecuted if they broke off such connections and refrained from "sabotage and counter-revolution."

7.) That a Chinese military and administrative commission and a military headquarters would be set up in Tibet to carry out the terms of the Agreement.

Thus, Peking gained by both force and the show of force full control of Tibet. The Chinese government took over Tibet's external affairs, communications, and trade. The Chinese Communist People's Liberation Army decided to absorb the Tibetan army; Tibet was granted "regional autonomy" within the confines of the new sovereignty of Communist China. The fictitious nature of the autonomy to be enjoyed by Tibet was soon made clear, as we shall see presently.

Once the Chinese Communists took over Tibet, students of Communism realized, as did the Tibetans themselves, that it would be only a matter of months before Peking began to Communize the country. While China took a series of unwarranted measures to integrate Tibet into Communist China, she continued, for propaganda purposes, to assure the Dalai Lama and his government that she would respect Tibet's autonomy and guarantee the integrity of Tibetan political and religious institutions.

In 1952 the Chinese authorities divided Tibet into three administrative areas and established a separate military command for the country. The central and western portions of Tibet were placed under the administration of the Dalai Lama; the Shigatse area under the Panchen Lama; and the eastern region under a Chinese general. Thus the Dalai Lama's secular and political authority and jurisdiction were reduced to a quarter of what they had been.

Peking began to open up Tibet. Two national highways linking the country with China were built, and airfields were constructed in at least three areas. The traditional southern direction of Tibetan trade was turned toward China, and hundreds of Tibetan students were recruited for Communist orientation, indoctrination, and technical training in Peking.

On April 20, 1954, the government of India signed an agreement with the Chinese Communist Government on the relations between India and Tibet. In this Agreement, the government of India for the first time recognized Tibet as the "Tibet region of China" and not as "autonomous Tibet." This was a tacit acceptance of Chinese sovereignty over Tibet. This Agreement was designed to safeguard the traditional trade and cultural intercourse between India and Tibet and to facilitate travel and pilgrimages between the two countries. In fact, it was this Agreement that formulated for the first time the much publicized and now famous "Five Principles of Coexistence"—*Pancha Sheela*—that were supposed to govern and guide the relations between India and China.

While this Agreement may or may not have opened a new chapter in the history of Sino-Indian relations, it certainly sealed the fate of Tibet and her people as an independent entity and left them at the mercy of the Chinese Communist Government. As was to be discovered later, the Chinese had no intention of respecting the autonomy of Tibet and her particular religious way of life. And soon after this Agreement, India found that the Communization and militarization of Tibet had seriously begun, jeopardizing the security and tranquillity of her northeastern border. But with the signing of the Sino-Indian agreement on Tibet, China disposed of India's special interest in Tibet and turned her attention to open and overt measures to bring Tibet into line.

While the Sino-Tibetan Agreement specifically mentioned

that the "Tibetan Regional Government would *voluntarily*
carry out reforms without interference from the Chinese,"
the Chinese government decided to launch land reforms
and collectivize land in Tibet, land that had belonged for
centuries to lamaseries and monasteries. With the "nationali-
zation" of these lands, the monasteries lost their revenue and
could not carry on their religious activities. The Tibetans
became suspicious that Peking was out to destroy their
religious way of life. This led to a major revolt in 1956,
news of which leaked out and received wide publicity abroad
but none in China. Military measures were taken to suppress
the revolt, and it was later reported that the revolt was
serious enough for the Chinese to have bombed some Tibetan
villages, killing some thousands of Tibetans.

Another major revolt broke out in the spring of 1957—a
revolt which the Chinese admitted, but only as a revolt of
"Tibetan counter-revolutionary bandits." Of course, anyone
who is against the Peking regime is both a bandit and a
counter-revolutionary.

For the next two years, that is, until the 1959 large-scale
revolt broke out, the Chinese Communists tried to go slow,
for the Party had decided that Tibet "was not yet ripe for
socialism."

But when all Peking's pressure and persuasion continued
to make little or no impression on the Tibetan people and
government, the Communists resorted to the more drastic
tactics of altering the very ethnic composition of Tibet's
population. While the Communists talked of the *cultural
autonomy* of her "nationalities" (or rather "national minorities"), they carried out policies designed eventually to reduce Tibetans to a minority in their own country by settling
thousands of Chinese (Han) immigrants in Tibet.

This was in keeping with the Communist policy of not
only colonizing and populating all frontier areas of China,
but also altering the pattern of the distribution of ethnic
and religious minorities in the country. Large colonies of

Chinese (Hans) have been settled in various parts of Tibet, and it is these immigrants and alien Chinese that now occupy all key positions in the political and economic life of the country. It is possible that within a decade Tibetans may well become a minority in their own country. All these and more provocations have contributed to the spread of wide disaffection toward the Communist rule. These smoldering embers of suspicion and distrust eventually burst into the flames of a national uprising, described earlier in this chapter.

VI

What of the future? It is to be earnestly hoped that real and lasting peace will soon be restored in Tibet and that there will be no need for further bloodshed. When peace does return, serious efforts should be made by countries like India to restore the Dalai Lama to his rightful place in Lhasa, and, what is more important, to restore Tibet to her former free cultural and political status. It is realized that this is more easily said than done.

The United Nations apparently can do little, for beyond a formal, verbal censure, how can the U.N. bring order to a country which is not a member? And Peking has repeatedly revealed her indifference to the U.N.'s opinion and, for that matter, to the larger and more compelling world public opinion. India could play a vital role here, but unfortunately she is bound by the self-imposed limitations of the avowed objectives of her own foreign policy. There is certainly a need for some reorientation in India's foreign policy.

No matter what the eventual outcome of the Tibetan revolt, it has taught all the uncommitted Asian countries a very useful lesson on the nature and objectives of Communism in general and Chinese Communism in particular. Asia has fought relentlessly for nearly a century to overthrow Western imperialism, *not* to fall victim to another and more menacing imperialism—Communism. The fact that this new colonialism is cloaked under revolutionary slogans of "people's revolution" and "socialist progress" should not deceive anyone. As the Indian leader Mr. Jayaprakash Narain pointed out: "In Tibet we see at this moment the workings of a new imperialism which is far more dangerous than the old because it marches under the banner of a so-called revolutionary ideology."

It is a strange kind of a people's revolution that extols the Chinese love of China with intense pride but denies the Tibetans' love for Tibet. But this is not so strange to those who are familiar with Communist ways. Russians must love Russia, but Hungarians must not love Hungary. Tibetan patriots are criminals just as Hungarian patriots are criminals. In Russia, patriotic love for the motherland is laudable, but, in the satellite countries, love must not be for the motherland but for the superior ideological mother— International Communism. There are some countries where this truth has not yet been grasped. Indian Communists, for instance, are not bothered in the least about the security of India's frontiers, but they are very much concerned about Communist China's rights in Tibet.

The Communists all over the world must realize that it is too late in the day to resurrect imperialism, no matter under what new name it is imposed. The colonial people of the world have put up a long and tiring fight to regain their freedom from the old Western European imperialism of the British, French, Dutch, etc., and have largely succeeded, though vestiges of the old imperialism still continue in Africa. And the world today is not in a mood to tolerate the old or new forms of imperialism, whether it is the Anglo-French attempt to take Suez, the Russian suppression of the Hungarian demand for freedom, or China's imposition of Communism on Tibet.

And last, no country has any right to impose "progress"— even granting that Chinese Communism can be so described

—on countries which do not want it. It is true that Tibet is economically and socially a backward country, and more theocratic than secular. But every country should have the right to lead and preserve her way of life, no matter how obscurantist it may appear to others, so long as she is peaceful and does not encroach upon the rights of others.

China is bound to realize sooner or later that, in gaining Tibet, she has lost Asia.

9

Sino-Indian Relations

A country's foreign policy is generally governed by numerous historical, political, economic, geographic, cultural, religious, ethnic, and other considerations. But the main motivation is really enlightened self-interest. Through the centuries this has been true of every country in the world which has had anything like a foreign policy. However, this does not mean that a nation's foreign policy, because it is governed by self-interest, need necessarily be Machiavellian and bereft of any ennobling idealism. While the Indian government conducts its foreign affairs on the principle of what is good for India as the policy-makers understand it, there are certain progressive and theoretical principles upon which every foreign policy action is based. We may not always succeed in our aims, and sometimes we fall far short of them, especially when conflicting interests arise; nevertheless, the objectives are there, not as an ornamental façade but as serious guide posts.

An objective and non-partisan evaluation of India's foreign policy during the last dozen years will reveal that her efforts have been directed in the main to the promotion of peace, even if peace is negatively defined as the sum total of averted and arrested wars. Whether it is in Indonesia or among the emerging states of Indochina, in Israel or Korea, Egypt or Tibet, or with Pakistan, or in the general East-West cold war, India's sole aim has been to lessen international tensions, assist in putting out regional conflagrations, localize conflicts, and act as an honest mediator when invited to do so. India has, I believe, played the useful role of peacemaker unobtrusively and unostentatiously, and without thrusting herself into every international disagreement as a professional neutral. And future historians of our times may not be wrong if they conclude that India has been, by and large, successful in her peacemaking role during these difficult years.

This magnificent devotion to peace is all the more significant when it is remembered that India (like the United States of America) has not been in recent decades a bloody theater of war, as Europe, Japan, and China have been. But it is understandable in view of India's cultural heritage and the unique, non-violent way in which she has regained her lost political freedom. For India's policy of promoting international peace is not just an abstract theoretical principle which has accidentally commended itself into adoption. It has a deeper national content. It is in a way the culmination of thousands of years of Indian tradition—a tradition of tolerance and understanding which has evolved through the difficult centuries of the cultural evolution which have made India into a fairly successful melting pot of different ethnic, cultural, and religious strains. It is not a hot-house plant, this passion of India's for peace, but an extension of Buddhist and Gandhian ideals of non-violence and pacifism.

While it is true that the Indian government does not believe in a policy of non-violence and pacifism (and what government does?), I believe that the average citizen of India is a quasi-pacifist at heart; he has a horror of war and all it implies, and he believes strongly in a policy of live and let live. It is because of this primary objective of promoting peace which India has so consistently followed that her voice has come to command certain respect and weight in the council of nations disproportionate to her importance on the basis of national income, industrial power, or the strength of her defense forces.

The second major aim behind India's foreign policy is the abolition of colonialism and the hastening of political freedom for all subject peoples. Today no argument need be advanced in support of self-government. Political freedom is the birthright of all peoples, no matter what the stage of their cultural evolution. This policy is also understandable, for our memories of being a subject nation are still with us. And consequently our sympathies are with the colonial peoples in their struggles for emancipation. While European imperialism has almost disappeared from Asia, the old colonialism, in all its medieval crudeness, still persists in parts of Africa. And our moral support has always been with the African and other colonial peoples in their struggle for freedom.

India's Good Neighbor Policy is our third general principle. We want to be at peace and live in friendship with every nation, no matter what its internal political system or economic ideology, whether the country is a neighbor with whom we have close ties and a common frontier or a country as remote as Chile.

It is against the background of these general principles, and in a sense as an extension of them, that *Pancha Sheela* was formulated. These "Five Principles of Coexistence" are: 1.) Mutual respect for each other's territorial integrity and sovereignty; 2.) Non-aggression; 3.) Non-interference in each other's internal affairs; 4.) Equality and mutual advantage; and 5.) Peaceful coexistence and economic cooperation.

While it is true that every issue of our foreign policy is examined on its merits, these in general have been the guiding principles of our foreign policy. And the consistent architect of this progressive neutralism, which draws admiration as well as criticism from both ideological fronts, is the Prime Minister—Pandit Nehru. The essential correctness and sanity of this policy is underlined when one finds that it is sometimes attacked both by the Western democracies and by the Communist countries. The West has accused Prime Minister Nehru of being a "fellow traveler," and Russia and China have called him "a running dog of imperialism." India's neutrality must really be effective if she is attacked from both sides!

Neutralism does not mean the negation of ideals. India believes in a democratic, parliamentary, and representative form of government. She believes in all the freedoms of the Western liberal tradition. And among the countries that have emerged free after World War II, India alone continues to maintain a democratic and stable government, registering steady economic and social progress. She has neither sacrificed her ideals of freedom and democracy nor has she jumped into the cold war in the name of destroying Communism.

How have these general principles of India's foreign policy governed her relations with China? Some ancient and recent facts of Sino-Indian relations are worth recalling.

India and China are among the world's most ancient cultures, with much in common in art and literature, religious forms, and social institutions. These two most populous nations of the world are the major architects and inheritors of what may be roughly called the Asian way of life—a way of life that once attached more importance to matters of the spirit and less to material welfare. Both evolved superior cultures which continuously adapted themselves to successive internal dissensions and external onslaughts. But neither India nor China was able to defend itself against the military attacks of Western nations. And as a result both countries suffered political humiliation and subjection at the hands of European imperialists. It was only an historical accident that made India the private preserve of a single power, Britain, while China became the prey of the rival imperialisms of Britain, France, Germany, Japan, and Russia. While India reaped from her political subjection and economic exploitation such gains as peace and stability, a well-ordered administration, and a utilitarian exposure to Western science and culture and British political ideals and institutions, China, in the spurious name of national sovereignty, remained a stagnant and semicolonial country, with neither peaceful conditions nor a stable government. Thus, when India became free in 1947, she was far more advanced administratively, culturally, and materially than was China in 1949 after her Liberation.

II

For more than two thousand years India has had some link or other with China, and her relations have been peaceful through the centuries for the simple reason that no area of conflict between the two countries ever arose. Actually, thanks to a 2,500-mile rugged and near-impassable frontier, running along a most difficult terrain, India and China have not had too much to do with each other except for the major cultural factor of Buddhism. Buddha has made China India's debtor. India sent such dedicated Buddhist missionaries as Gobharana and Kashyapa Matanga to China during the reign of Emperor Ming-ti of the Han Dynasty. And with the export of Buddhism, India began to import pilgrims from China. During the reign of Chandragupta Maurya in the fourth century, India received Fa Hsien, the celebrated Chinese pilgrim. Three centuries later, when Harsha was on the throne of India, Hsuan Tsang visited the country. Their chronicles are a precious source of Indian history and bear witness to the cultural interflow between the two countries. And though with the aggressive arrival of Islam in Central and Southern Asia, about the tenth century, active connections between the two countries ceased, commerce and trade continued to thrive between them. But during the next few centuries each became preoccupied with political troubles and various foreign invaders; and only in recent decades has a new political consciousness and a sense of Asian solidarity emerged. Now the two countries have rediscovered each other under altered and rather difficult circumstances.

Since China's Communist revolution, India has not only recognized the new regime but has tried to promote Sino-Indian friendship in every possible way. But peace requires understanding, and such understanding can arise only from respect for and authentic and reliable knowledge of each other's way of life. And in this matter, China, or any Communist country for that matter, can never be fair, for it has nothing but contempt for the "decadent" and "degenerate" countries of capitalism. India concedes that China can have Communism or any outmoded system she wants and that it is her internal affair. But Communist China does not really concede that India's political and economic institutions are India's private concern, and, what is more, the Chinese believe that it is their duty to "liberate" India from her bourgeois and reactionary rulers and give her the blessings of "democratic dictatorship." A careful perusal of Communist writings, particularly of the Chinese even after 1947 when India became politically free, reveals that, though the Comintern has been abolished, the missionary zeal of the Communists to seek new converts has not lessened. The amount of money, energy, and time the Communist countries expend in other countries in open as well as devious ways to foment discontent, stir up trouble, and lay the foundations for revolution is enormous. Thus one of the principles of *Pancha Sheela*—that of non-interference in internal affairs—has never really been in effect. While the Indian government knows this, the average citizen in India does not appear to be aware of it.

Secondly, on the question of promoting knowledge of each other's way of life, China has been less than honest. This is not surprising, when we remember that her interest is not in understanding the Indian way of life but in undermining it. China's failure to provide her people with correct knowledge about India is not accidental but deliberate.

While Chinese politicians and officials have in the past talked incessantly of "cultural interflow" between the two countries, there is very little knowledge in China of India, her problems, or her achievements. As the Chinese newspapers, magazines, and other mass media are strictly government-controlled, this ignorance can only be understood as deliberately imposed on the people by their totalitarian regime. Indian newspapers carry a great deal more news of China than Chinese newspapers do of India. In India, there is a continuous coverage of the Chinese point of view even when such views are inimical to her. Thanks to the Indian Communist Party and its well-known, if not sufficiently appreciated, extraterritorial and supranational loyalty, the Chinese Communist point of view does not lack spokesmen in India. But in China, any point of view other than the Communists' is not tolerated.

This lack of news—or perhaps the supply of an occasional misleading item about India in the Chinese press—has not been exactly the best way of promoting "cultural interflow." Major national events have been ignored and some obscure utterances of inconsequential Indian Communists highlighted. A new factory in formerly Communist Kerala (under India's Five-Year Plans) received more publicity as a *Communist* achievement than other and much more important happenings elsewhere in India.

I asked a student leader in Peking what he knew of India and her leaders. "If I am right," he said, "there are two Indias. In the north, capitalist India, Mr. Nehru is the Prime Minister and he is friendly to us. [This, of course, was before the Tibetan revolt and China's assault on India's frontier.] And in the southern half, Kerala, Mr. Namboodiripad is the Prime Minister. And the southern government is a People's Government like ours." And when the student was informed by our interpreter that I was from the south, he pumped my hand profusely and welcomed me to the campus most warmly as a fellow comrade! This is only a random

sample, but during my travels in China I found this mis-
information about India by no means an isolated example.
The people were already beginning to think of India in
terms of a partitioned Korea or a Vietnam. It is wishful
thinking, but it is there.

When I went around the new and impressive iron and
steel plant constructed by the Russians at Wuhan, the Director gave me a learned running commentary on all that was
going on, and he appeared to be well informed about steel.
Later, while talking about steel production in India, he
asked me how the steel plant being set up by the Russians
at Bhilai was coming along. I told him that it was progressing
quite well and was expected to go into production soon. He
was full of praise for the "selfless help" of the Soviet Union
in starting the first real steel plants in both China and India.
I told him that the Russian steel plant was not our first and
that West Germany was helping us to build one at Rourkela
in Orissa and the British were also helping to build one
at Durgapur in Bengal. He was very much surprised that
India would shortly have three new steel plants, and when
I told him that these would be in addition to the three we
already have—that the Tatas had been producing steel for
the last fifty years at Jamshedpur in Bihar, and that we
had plants at Calcutta (Indian Iron and Steel) and Mysore
(Bhadravathi), the Director looked frankly skeptical. "But
I thought the Russians were setting up the *first* steel plant
in India!" he said. There was an exchange in Chinese among
his colleagues, after which he fell silent.

A similar incident occurred at the State Film Studios in
Shanghai, where I was invited to a private showing of some
Chinese films. Here again the head of the studios knew
little about India's enormous progress in the film industry
as a private enterprise.

This ignorance in China of India's progress raises many
questions. The Chinese press, of course, does not say much
about India's advancement because India does not belong

to the Communist camp and her achievements are not the outcome of a Communist system. Numerous Indian delegations have visited China and returned to India with rosy pictures of Red achievements; but their Chinese counterparts who have visited India obviously do not on their return to China report any of *India's* achievements. At any rate there is no account of them in the Chinese press.

What is worse, the average Indian citizen has been misled by the reports of Indian visitors to China for, with very few exceptions, these visitors have presented only one side of the Chinese picture. We have heard only of China's achievements—such as they are—without any reference to the enormous human price paid for them. The curious reason for this appears to be that, since the Indian government was friendly with China, no one should say anything against China. The Indian government is friendly with countless other countries, but this does not seem to deter Indians from criticizing certain aspects of these countries. An Indian scientist who visited China some time ago confided to me the other day that he agreed with all that I had said on China and that my impressions confirmed his own, but he himself did not want to say such things as they might be shocking to public opinion in India! And I in turn am shocked that friendship with China should mean that we must suppress the truth. We should be all for understanding and co-existence. But the need in a democracy to place truth and one's honest opinion before the public, no matter what current official and other attitudes may be, cannot be over-emphasized.

This indiscriminate adulation of Red China led, as one might expect, to a denigration of India. It became fashionable in certain circles to criticize the Indian government and to show little or no appreciation of the progress that free India has been able to register during the last twelve years. Even outside observers have conceded that India has taken important strides toward a better deal for the average man.

But this undue praise of China and the invidious comparison with India implied that the country's free and democratic government, with its mixed economy, was not able to deliver the goods.

This unflattering comparison of India's record with that of China had another ironical aspect. It gave impetus to the activities of the Indian Communist Party to undermine the Indian government. The Indian government, which was largely responsible for the spread of such a rosy picture of China, could hardly blame the electorate for voting the Communists of Kerala into power. In this sense, the Indian government seemed to be unconsciously working at cross purposes. Indians were friendly and helpful and full of admiration for the foreign Communists, and the indigenous ones reaped the reflected glory.

III

At the time of this writing, relations between India and China have considerably deteriorated. For some years now, India has been protesting to China against the publication and circulation of certain maps showing considerable chunks of Indian territory along the Sino-Indian and Indo-Tibetan frontier as Chinese. When I was in China, I raised this question with some important officials, but I received the uniform reply that these were old maps published during the Kuomintang regime and had not been put out by the present People's Government. To my question why, when everything else done during the "Chiang clique" regime had been changed, the present government had not thought fit to publish correct maps, especially since the present old maps were offensive to a friendly country, I received no reply. Thus, in a way, the border dispute has been there in a latent fashion ever since the Communists came to power. And it is difficult to understand why the Indian government did not demand an immediate categorical answer on this question from Peking during the days of romantic friendship.

China claims two huge chunks of Indian territory on the Sino-Indian border as Chinese. On the northeast, between India and Tibet, the traditional frontier is based on the McMahon Line. This, as pointed out in our discussion of Tibet, is the 800-mile border between India and Tibet drawn some fifty years ago at the Simla Conference by Sir A. H. McMahon, who represented Britain. Now Peking states that this traditional frontier, which has never been questioned before, was never formally ratified by any Chinese government. Peking further accuses India of complicity with British imperialism because the McMahon Line was essentially a product of British deliberations. It is not the fault of India that the then Chinese government had no time, preoccupied as she was with internal troubles, to register doubts about the border as it was then drawn.

And Peking forgets, of course, that India, as a successor government to the British in India, inherited the duties and responsibilities of the former government. However, should there be any agreement about the present demarcation of the frontier, a civilized government would be expected to raise the question through the regular diplomatic channels and to discuss and settle the matter to its satisfaction. But what China (a supposedly friendly China and a China which has been consistently championed by India during the last decade to the dismay of America and other Western nations friendly to India) has done is unilaterally to repudiate the accepted, traditional frontier. Peking has not repudiated the frontier for any minor adjustments, but blandly claims some 35,000 square miles of India's Northeast Frontier Agency as belonging to China. And China has not stopped with this. She has resorted to violence and has forcibly occupied Longju, the Indian frontier post. This is Communist existence but certainly not coexistence! India has met this Chinese show of strength with patience and restraint and with nothing more than diplomatic protests. This civilized restraint on the part of India is possibly interpreted by China as political weakness.

The second area of the Sino-Indian border dispute is in Ladakh along the 1,100-mile-long Kashmir-Tibet frontier. Here there is no treaty or any formal declaration beyond what time, convention, and accepted usage have sanctified as the border between Indian Kashmir and Tibet. There has never been any dispute about this border in the past between the erstwhile Maharajas of Kashmir and the British government in India on the one hand, or the Tibetan authorities and the Chinese government on the other.

According to a government of India release, of this 1,100-mile-long frontier between Kashmir and Tibet, "about 300 miles of the extreme Western sector is covered by the territory of Kashmir which is now illegally occupied by Pakistan. The major part of Kashmir's frontiers with China runs along a well-defined watershed, and the eastern section in particular has been recognized by custom for over three centuries. It was also confirmed by treaties signed between Ladakh and Tibet. This boundary includes in India the whole of the Aksai Chin plateau, the Changchengmo valley, and other areas. However, Chinese maps have been showing the boundary in this area much farther west so as to include about 6,000 square miles—the greater part of Aksai Chin and parts of Changchengmo valley and other areas in Tibet."

What astonishes one is that China at no time demanded from India this territory, which she claims as her own, in any formal manner. She ignored the traditional frontier, trespassed more than forty miles into Indian territory, and built a 100-mile-long road through the eastern part of Aksai Chin. The Chinese now do not just *claim* this huge chunk of Indian area; they have occupied it, and what is more they are controlling the region effectively enough to arrest as trespassers Indian parties in 1958 and 1959. These outrageous actions on the part of the Chinese resulted in nothing more than "polite but strong" protests from India.

Relations between Delhi and Peking reached a crisis when the news arrived at the end of October, 1959, that Indian and Chinese troops had clashed. At Hot Springs in Ladakh district, some forty-five miles from the Kashmir-Tibet border, when two Indian constables of the Indian Frontier Patrol did not return to their camp, a searching party of fifty Indians went out to look for them. From a hilltop, the Chinese troops opened fire without inquiry or reason. The Indians fired back, but they were subdued by grenades and mortar. Nine Indian constables were killed and ten were captured.

This incident is probably the worst clash that has occurred as yet between the Indians and Chinese as a result of the border dispute. It roused the entire Indian nation, which demanded quick and effective retaliation. Newspapers asked for cessation of diplomatic relations. Even leading members of the Congress Party (the party in power) demanded that something should be done to save India's honor and her territorial integrity. All political parties and groups voiced their sudden awareness of this new Communist menace on the nation's northern frontiers. But the Indian Communist Party alone stood out shamelessly true to its tradition of supranational loyalties and defended China's rights over Indian territory! Nehru pleaded for restraint but promised an angry and disillusioned nation that force, if necessary, would be used to eject the Chinese Communists who have trespassed into and occupied Indian territory. The 2,500-mile-long frontier from northwest Kashmir to the junction of the India-Burma-China frontiers has now been turned over to the Indian military authorities.

Nehru's trust in the Chinese Communist leaders has been betrayed, just as some of us had predicted it would be, and the Indian government's foreign policy of neutrality and friendship with Communist China has become suspect. Does this mean, in the last analysis, that India's neutral foreign policy has failed? All that can be said is that Prime Minister Nehru, with the best intentions in the world and with an ardent desire to promote peace, took a plunge in trusting Communist China. The trust has been misplaced, and, since these incidents may recur in the future, it is time for India's foreign policy toward China to be changed.

These disputes over maps and frontiers are only symptoms; the disease of Communist ideology is a deep-seated one. The real struggle of the future in Asia will not be between India and China as such but between democracy and freedom on the one hand and Communism and its tyranny on the other. Asia's destiny will be mortgaged on the outcome of this ideological struggle. It will be a sad day for Asia if, after a struggle of two centuries, she overthrows European imperialism only to become the victim of another and more sinister imperialism—Communism.

10
India, China, and Asia

Asia, perhaps the oldest of the continents, is, in a geo-political sense, the center of the world. Geographically, Europe is her annex, Africa her subcontinent, and Australia her island. Asia is also the home of some of the oldest cultures in the world and almost all the major religions. And, of the many cultures evolved by various ethnic-national groups, two dominant cultures, those of India and China, have come down to this day, continuous and unbroken, with a tradition stretching back more than 5,000 years. While several comparable cultures and civilizations have risen in other parts of the world, the tradition of continuity in the face of internal disturbances and external onslaught is nowhere so marked as in India and China.

Asian culture and civilization were fundamentally un-touched by the West up to the end of the eighteenth century, some three hundred years after the voyage of Vasco da Gama had opened up the Indian Ocean and Asia to European navigation and exploration. However, because of European expansionism and because of the internal struggles for po-litical power in various Asian countries and their lack of military strength, half of Asia had come under European rule by the middle of the nineteenth century. The rivalry between the European powers in Asia was so keen that few Asian countries escaped direct political domination by the West, and those that did escape found themselves in the role of buffer states. Some Asian countries lost their freedom entirely; others enjoyed a spurious sovereignty; all were subject to strong economic, political, and cultural pres-sures from the West. In short, they had no genuine inde-pendence.

This subjugation also had its positive aspects. On the one hand, the loss of political freedom and of the opportunity for economic development was accompanied by Western notions of racial superiority and cultural exclusiveness. On the other hand, reacting to prejudice and discrimination, Asia began to take great pride in her own traditional cultures and to adapt them to the needs of the twentieth century.

Asia lost her political and economic freedom. At the same time she was introduced to Western science and technology and imbibed European liberal democratic traditions. It must be said to the credit of the Europeans that, whatever their motives in coming to Asia, they brought with them the fruits of the scientific, medical, and political revolutions that were so radically changing the life of Western man. And it was these revolutions that led to the eventual liquidation of European imperialism in Asia.

Three substantial colonial empires—those of Britain, France, and Holland—collapsed within a decade and a half of the termination of World War II. Russia, Japan, and the United States had had their own colonies in Asia; though these were of a different vintage, they too have disappeared forever. The United States gave freedom to the Philippines, fulfilling her own promise. Japan's empire was taken away after her defeat in World War II. And the Russian empire was liquidated by the Communist Revolution, a revolution that many hoped would usher in a new civilization.

Today, every country in Asia, with the minor exceptions of Goa, Hong Kong, Kowloon, Macao, Borneo, and a few other islands, has become free.

The fight for national political freedom from Western European imperialism was led, through example and implication, by India under the guidance of Gandhi. While India's neighboring countries produced no Gandhis, the Indian national movement was by and large responsible for arousing the latent nationalist sentiment in the rest of

Asia, and particularly in Southeast Asia. And thus it was largely as a by-product of India's fight against Britain that India's neighbors became free.

When Asian colonial countries were fighting for political freedom, subject peoples of all ideological persuasions made common cause. No matter what an Asian's economic belief or philosophy, he knew that the paramount problem was one of self-government and political liberty. He realized that freedom was not an end in itself but an essential objective, for only in freedom could Asians hope to raise their standard of living and join the battle against poverty, ignorance, and disease.

With the arrival of freedom, one would have expected a clash between contending economic ideologies. But the debate in the liberated Asian countries was not confined merely to economic systems. It deepened into a struggle between Communism as a total philosophy embracing every field of human endeavor, on the one hand, and freedom on the other. And thus began the real battle for postwar Asia.

In this battle Communism enjoys an immediate advantage because it is a new force, a phenomenon of unknown dimensions. In the Asian mind there remains the strong association of the West with detested colonialism. It may seem shocking to the American and European that colonialism could hold greater misery and unhappiness in Asian eyes than Communism, but colonialism has been a matter of bitter personal, national, and racial experience. Asia has not yet had time to forget her wounds.

Asian nationalists have too recently emerged from their battle with the former monster, colonialism, to view the new monster, Communism, clearly. Communism promises them acceptance and equality, whereas apartheid, Notting Hill, Little Rock, and Baton Rouge, widely discussed in the Asian press, seem to confirm the West's continuing denial of racial equality and score heavily against the West in its propaganda battle with Communism.

The new Asia is at the crossroads. She wants to catch up with the advanced West in political stability, economic advancement, and cultural progress. Which is the best and quickest method, the democratic way or the Communist way? Which will deliver the goods? Which will preserve and enhance human values? Does Asia want rapid economic development at tremendous human cost? Or can we assure an ever-rising standard of living to the underprivileged millions without destroying basic human values? India and China represent to Asia the two conflicting ideologies of democracy and Communism, and their progress is being carefully watched by the emergent nations of Asia and Africa.

II

What has India's record been during the last dozen years of her political freedom? Only the briefest review of India's political integration, economic planning and development, and social progress is possible here.

A few basic facts: India occupies an area two-fifths the size of the continental United States of America and shelters a total of 438,000,000 people—more than double the population of the United States of America, or a seventh of mankind. Because of a rapid decline in mortality and an increase in life expectancy, India's population is now increasing by about 2 per cent a year, and at this rate of increase her population may reach some 500,000,000 by 1970. India is the largest nation in the non-Communist world.

India's political record since independence has been a commendable one. Her democratic constitution combines the best features of the British and American constitutions.

It guarantees freedom of speech, press, and worship, protects the rights of minorities, and establishes the rule of law and an independent judiciary. It grants equal status to women and equal recognition to all religions despite the overwhelming predominance of Hinduism. It has outlawed untouchability and banned many archaic and unjust customs which had the sanction of ancient tradition and custom. India has had two general elections and a third is scheduled for 1962. In each of the last two elections, nearly a dozen political parties contested, and more than 100,000,000 people registered their votes. Some 45 per cent of these voters were women.

Another significant internal development has been the political integration of the country. Under British rule there were quasi-autonomous British provinces under British governors and 544 semi-autonomous Indian states, most of them feudal and ruled by maharajas. When India became free, these princely states were integrated into the rest of the country without bloodshed or violence. This integrated territory of India has recently been reorganized into fifteen states on the principles of linguistic unity and administrative convenience.

India has chosen to remain in the Commonwealth, though she fought Great Britain bitterly, if non-violently, for more than half a century. She has no racial, linguistic, or cultural ties with Britain and her overseas daughter communities. But India's entry into the Commonwealth has pioneered the change of the British Commonwealth into a non-racial, non-regional, and, by and large, non-doctrinaire association of free peoples which is held together by historic ties, sentimental loyalties, and certain moral ideals.

In the area of economic development, the crux of India's problem, she has been registering steady progress. The nation under the leadership of Nehru has opted for a "socialistic pattern of society," a term which has led to some misunderstanding both in India and abroad. In India, the term means a mixed economy where private and public enterprise work together in a democratic framework to lessen the great gulf between the small minority of "haves" and the vast multitude of "have nots." There is nothing dogmatic or doctrinaire about Indian socialism; it is simply humanism.

To assure every man, woman, and child in India the basic necessities of life, India has employed careful economic planning. In practice, India operates under a mixed economy, with the government assuming over-all responsibility for planning the development of industry and for its regulation in the larger interests of the nation. The industries that are publicly sponsored are the defense industries, atomic energy, iron and steel (private enterprise has a significant share in iron and steel), aircraft, railways, and shipbuilding. These are also the industries which need tremendous capital not readily available to private enterprise. A large and growing field, however, is left open to private investment— the manufacture of textiles, aluminum, cement, machine tools, and chemical and pharmaceutical products among others. While opinion exists in India that private enterprise does not receive all the encouragement it deserves, it is undeniable that the present convenient, if perhaps arbitrary, division between public and private enterprise has markedly accelerated India's large-scale and heavy industrialization.

The policy of promoting industrialization at a rapid pace is designed to create new employment opportunities that will siphon off surplus population from the overcrowded soil to urban factories. New urban patterns of living may in time reduce the birth rate and thus contribute to the solution of India's population problem. In addition, India has embarked upon a democratic, voluntary policy of population control unlike Communist China's Marxist-oriented pro-natalist policy.

To achieve the transformation from an economy of scarcity into an economy of sufficiency, if not eventual abundance, India has mapped out Five-Year Plans. She has successfully completed two of these and is on the eve of embarking upon a third.

The main objective of the first Five-Year Plan was to assure an adequate supply of food and consumer goods for the period of intensive industrial development that lay ahead. The major part of the Plan's outlay, about $5,000,000,000, was used for the development of agriculture and transport and for vast irrigation, flood-control, and hydroelectric projects. The remaining capital, along with almost $1,000,-000,000 of private capital, was spent largely on light industry.

The second Five-Year Plan, which came into force in 1956, sought to increase the national income by 25 per cent and aimed at rapid industrialization, particularly of basic and heavy industries, at a considerable increase in employment opportunities, and at a reduction of inequalities in income and wealth. The Plan has come close to fulfillment, but certain targets dependent on the availability of external finance have had to be revised.

In the social and religious spheres, India has registered almost spectacular progress, despite the complex structures and divisive forces she has had to deal with.

By virtue of her historical traditions of tolerance, India has sheltered all the chief religions of mankind; now although Hinduism is practiced by an overwhelming majority of the population, Moslems, Christians, Sikhs, Buddhists, Jains, Parsis, and others form small but important minorities. According to her constitution (and unlike Pakistan, which is a theocratic state), India is a secular republic where all religious groups have equality before the law.

In addition to the various religious communities, linguistic groups also divide India. The constitution recognizes fourteen major languages, and the people who speak them exhibit fierce loyalty to these languages and to the cultures that have arisen around them through the centuries. To encourage a peaceful and orderly growth on this basis, the country is organized administratively into linguistic provinces.

As important as the linguistic groups in their divisive influence and separatist tendencies are the various caste groups. But while the government is willing to preserve linguistic groups, it has begun to wage war against caste and its corollary of outcastes and untouchables. The constitution has outlawed untouchability, but the destruction of the caste system itself is not an easy task. It is hoped that with the steady increase of education, the growing number of intercaste marriages, and the growth of national and secular ideals, the system will weaken and die. Fortunately, the thoughtful citizen has already come to recognize the incompatibility of the caste system with democracy.

Thus India has embarked on numerous reforms that seek to integrate the country emotionally and to assure the welfare of the traditionally backward and underprivileged sections of the population within the framework of modern democracy. She is seeking political unity, economic development, and cultural synthesis without sacrificing her rich diversity or basic human values. And this is a record of which any country might be proud.

III

How does China's record during the last dozen years since her Communist revolution compare with India's in terms of material advancement and of human and spiritual values? The political, economic, and social development of the country since the revolution, has already been described in these pages. What is likely to be the effect on Asia of China's over-all development?

The two most significant facts to be remembered about China, in addition to her economic ideology, are the tremendous territory she covers and the massive size of her population. Geographically, she occupies a dominant position in east central Asia.

Politically, Mao and his men have been able to consolidate and stabilize their rule over a far-flung area in approximately a decade. Sinkiang (Chinese Turkestan) and Tibet, which were never an integral part of China under any regime in the past, have been conquered and annexed into China. There is always, of course, the fear that some group might rebel and wrest power from the Communists, just as they themselves seized political power from the Kuomintang. To avoid this possibility, they have liquidated every conceivable group that might some day oppose their regime. Whether it be individual landlords or an intellectual group, capitalists or Kuomingtang sympathizers—all have been silenced. The Communists have also established a national network of army units, party cells, and police stations, charged with the task of ensuring compliance with the directives of the ruling party.

In the structure and functions of the new government, the Communists have faithfully copied Russia. In both countries, the democratic façade is more elaborate and complete than in a real democracy. There are elections and voting. There is a parliament and debate. There are the President and Ministers and Governors. There are courts, judges, and law.

All these rituals are familiar to students of contemporary Communist countries. But China has made a special point of her elections and boasts universal adult franchise for all except counter-revolutionaries, unreformed capitalists and landlords, and political "criminals." No matter who does or does not vote, the results are a foregone conclusion. Communist elections, as Attlee pointed out long ago, are like a race with one horse. The Communist Party—the only party—chooses the only candidates for election. The word "election" loses its meaning when applied to this elaborate farce.

What are the major political objectives of Communist Chinese ideology and practice now that they have con-

quered the mainland and consolidated their military and
political power? Peace and coexistence on the one hand—
and territorial expansion on the other. And the Chinese see
nothing paradoxical about this.

Communist China is perhaps the best example in the
world today of Communist "double-talk" and "double-think"
policy. Visitors to China and students of her literature know
that everyone, from Mao to the man in the street, talks
about peace. The people, the press, the loudspeakers, the
entire propaganda machine scream incessantly about peace.
The Chinese want peace on the mainland, peace in Asia,
and peace in the whole world. Obviously it was "in pursuit
of peace" that the Communists fought a bloody thirty-year
civil war. In pursuit of the same objective, they fought in
Korea and are fighting for the offshore islands, not to speak
of Taiwan. Only to promote "peace," they annexed Tibet.
The current border disputes with India, Burma, Nepal, and
Bhutan, we are solemnly assured, are also directed toward
the same supreme ideal.

Privately, the leaders dismiss the possibility of peace or
peaceful coexistence as so much nonsense. They manufacture atomic weapons, increase the size of their armed
forces, and equip them with the latest weapons—all in the
name of resisting the much-publicized impending American
aggression. But to the world outside, China poses as the
living champion of peace. As an original signatory to *Pancha
Sheela*, China swears by coexistence (lulling unsuspecting
India into believing her for nearly a decade) and pleads
along with the Soviet Union against the manufacture, testing, and storage of atomic weapons as well as conventional
armaments.

The contradictions do not end here. Peaceful coexistence,
as spelled out in the Bandung Agreement, means the repu-
diation of violence and war as a means of settling international disagreements and controversial political issues, the
renunciation of interference in the internal affairs of other

countries, and the peaceful competition of rival socio-economic systems. But the Chinese struck the first blow against coexistence when they invaded Tibet, and now they maintain that war is inevitable as long as capitalism continues to exist anywhere in the world.

This then is how China seeks to achieve the first objective of her paradoxical policy—peace and coexistence. The Communists are now turning their attention to their second objective—ideological-cum-territorial expansion. The realization of this second objective is sought through propaganda, subversion, and, if necessary, military aid and intervention in Asia. Communist China undermines trust in existing non-Communist regimes, fans tensions between Communist and other parties, and promotes the creation of "people's democracies" in other countries. Ultimately, she hopes to build a satellite empire in Asia as the Soviet Union has done in Eastern Europe.

Chinese expansionism is nothing new, for historically every Chinese regime has sought to expand its frontiers whenever it had the necessary military power. From ancient times, the Chinese, through pressure of population on their limited and underdeveloped resources, have been pressing southward in search of food and shelter. The coastal and southern provinces have a long history of emigration, sometimes in violent hordes and sometimes peacefully. As merchants or moneychangers, peasants or petty shopkeepers, the Chinese have penetrated into every country that would receive them, and have successfully taken over a segment of their host's trade and commerce. The results of the expansion can be seen in the unassimilated Chinese minorities all over Southeast Asia—veritable states within states.

Communist China has not forgotten the old routes of Chinese expansion. The road is familiar—Tibet, Indochina, and the Himalayan borderlands. Even before she had begun to better her own standard of living, China started on her imperialist journey—North Korea, Tibet, North Vietnam,

Ladakh, Laos, etc. The planned attack goes on without any effective opposition. The Asians outside the Communist orbit have made no move to unite against the common enemy, and India, the major uncommitted nation of Asia, has given no leadership. In fact, China has been trying, with some success, to isolate India. To reach this end, and perhaps to lull the vigilance of prospective victims, she has convinced Afghanistan, Burma, and Nepal of her friendly and peaceful intentions. She has concluded agreements with Afghanistan and Nepal. And she has "adjusted" her borders with Burma by nibbling at Burmese territory.

In the light of these factors, two important questions must be examined. First, should Communist China be admitted into the United Nations? And, second, should India revise her foreign policy, make a new alignment, and take steps to prevent further Communist Chinese penetration into Asia?

IV

Should Communist China be admitted to the United Nations? This question has been on the agenda of the General Assembly for the last ten years, with the Soviet Union usually sponsoring China's admission and India consistently siding with Russia. This has been so during the years when China was trespassing into India (unknown to India and the world) and even during the last two or three years, when China's aggression against India has become a problem of acute concern in India.

Those who favor China's admission contend that she cannot be expected to comply with the rules of an international club of which she is not a member. But South Africa's treatment of her citizens of Indian origin, Russia's behavior in Hungary, and France's methods in Algeria indicate that United Nations membership does not necessarily provide a civilizing or reforming influence on its members. Furthermore, the eligibility of a nation for admission to the world body should depend on whether she is peace-loving, not on whether she stands in need of reform and correction. While seeking admission into the United Nations, Red China has continued to attack the world body and its Secretary-General and has shown scant respect for its objectives, decisions, and directives.

A second argument is that the only way to negotiate with China and deflect her from her present path of aggression, and thus reduce the risk of open war, is to admit her to the U.N. But the United States, Indonesia, and India, which have negotiated, or rather tried to negotiate, with Communist China, have discovered that the leaders of the Red regime will settle only on their own outrageous terms.

Another argument is that the United Nations should recognize the fact that the Communists are in effective control of the mainland. Therefore, it is contended, a denial of representation to Communist China is tantamount to ignoring the voice of more than 600,000,000 people. There is no doubt that the Peking regime controls the lives of all the mainland Chinese. But it must not be forgotten that the present rulers came to power after a long, bloody, and violent struggle. The Communists were not voted into power; they seized power through naked military force, and they are sustained through mass trials, political purges, and one-party dictatorship. During the first decade of their rule, Mao and his men have exterminated some 20,000,000 Chinese in the name of suppressing criminals and counter-revolutionaries, bandits and rebels—people who were really suspected of ideological opposition. Therefore, it is a moot question whether the regime reflects the real aspirations, longings, and wishes of the Chinese people.

Also to be considered is the loyalty of some 14,000,000 Chinese scattered over Southeast Asia. They are an influential but unassimilated part of the economic, political, and cultural life of such countries as Burma, Thailand, Malaya, Laos, Cambodia, Vietnam, Indonesia, and the Philippines.

Each of these countries must deal with the vexing problem of Chinese dual nationality, for the government in China, the Reds as well as their predecessors, has maintained that "a Chinese remains Chinese wherever he may be domiciled." No matter what the legal nationality of a Chinese, China regards him as her citizen. Today, many of these overseas Chinese look to Formosa as their spiritual home. But if Red China is admitted to the United Nations and thus elevated to a position of international respectability, it is reasonable to expect that the loyalty of the overseas Chinese will be redirected toward Peking.

The Chinese Communists ask whether their adherence to Communist ideology is the real barrier to their admission to the U.N. Since other Communist countries are members, it is clear that China is barred not merely because of her rival ideology and conflicting economic and political system. It is rather because of her deeds—deeds that have produced strain and tension, trouble and discord in areas where peace has prevailed for countless centuries. From northern Kashmir to South Korea, along a line of more than 6,000 miles, the Chinese Communists have promoted ideological disaffection and subversion, military aggression and conquest. This record deserves only one verdict; Communist China is untrustworthy. Like a two-faced Janus, she talks of peace while she stabs her neighbor in the back. Neither the prestige nor the power of the United Nations is likely to be enhanced by China's admission.

V

In the light of these disruptive factors, one must consider whether there is a need for a revision of India's foreign policy. It must be realized that a dozen years ago, when Prime Minister Nehru formulated the basic principles on which India's foreign policy was to be based, India as a free, modern state was barely two years old. In his formulation, a sound combination of idealism and national interest, the pursuit of peace was given the highest priority. As an under-developed nation, India had to maintain peace so that all her energies could be devoted to economic advancement. Consequently, the motto of Indian diplomacy was, and has continued to be, "Peace is worth the price of being mis-understood."

Perhaps the chief source of friction arising from this policy has been India's insistence that this peace be achieved "not through alignment with any major power or group of powers, but through an independent approach to each controversial or disputed issue." But this policy, it must be remembered, is not dissimilar to the foreign policy of the United States during the first century and a half of her existence.

During her first few years, India meticulously followed a policy of non-alignment. In the U.N., she voted with the United States and the other Western democracies as often as she did with the Soviet Union. But, of late, this course has proved increasingly futile. Sometimes literal neutrality appears to be a denial of principles—even the very principles India stands for. To some, there is no such thing as "strict neutrality." As an American wit asked recently: "Whose neutrals are they?" India's answer, of course, is that her neutrality is neither pro-West nor pro-East, but simply pro what she believes to be right. Unfortunately, the West con-siders us pro-East, and the East pro-West.

Our policy has also turned friends into enemies. Com-munist China—whose cause India espoused both within and without the United Nations, year in and year out—has turned bitterly anti-Indian.

Equally fruitless, to date, has been India's disagreement with Pakistan over Kashmir; Pakistan has not yet vacated the area she occupies. Furthermore, she has entered into a military pact that includes several countries demonstrably unsympathetic to India. Pakistan forms the western arm of SEATO, with Thailand in the center and the Philippines in the east. SEATO is ostensibly a mutual-security organization designed on a regional basis. But it has been boycotted by five nations of the region, led by the most important—India, whose opposition to all military alliances is well known. And such strength as SEATO has is derived from the five outside powers, the United States, Britain, France, Australia, and New Zealand. Since India has no ties with SEATO, she cannot expect to receive any help from it.

Nor is any uncommitted nation in Asia now in a position to help India in the unlikely event of Sino-Indian hostilities. All that fellow Asian neutrals could offer India would be polite condolences. Hence, there is plainly a compelling and immediate need for revising India's policy of neutrality and entering into new alliances that will strengthen her so that she may continue to grow and progress internally.

VI

The real and fundamental difference between Communist societies and democratic countries lies in the area of human freedom—the people's right to choose and change their own economic, political, and social systems as they like, to elect those who shall govern them within the framework of those systems, and "to enjoy, within that same framework, the civil liberties which relieve them of the fear of arbitrary injustice, permit them to practice freedom of the mind, and enable them to walk with their heads up." Therefore, the basic ideological issue before Asia is a struggle not between capitalism and socialism but between freedom and totalitarianism. The worker in the Soviet Union or China has no freedom, nor does he enjoy, in return for the loss of his freedom, a higher level of living than the workers in many "capitalist" countries. Under democratic capitalism, both abundance and freedom are possible.

The problem before Asia is to bring, within a reasonable period of time, both economic affluence and political freedom to those countries that have rejected Communism and have chosen the free way of life. It is not a question merely of the much-needed victory over poverty, but what is equally, if not more, important, of the *means* of achieving that victory.

Will India win the struggle of economic development through democracy and a mixed economy? Or will China win through Communist dictatorship and totalitarian regimentation? The postwar decade has witnessed the long-awaited liberation of all the colonial areas in Asia. But who will dominate the next and coming decades? India or China? What ideology will win the voluntary allegiance of a billion Asians? The answer depends to a considerable extent on America's role in India's economic development.